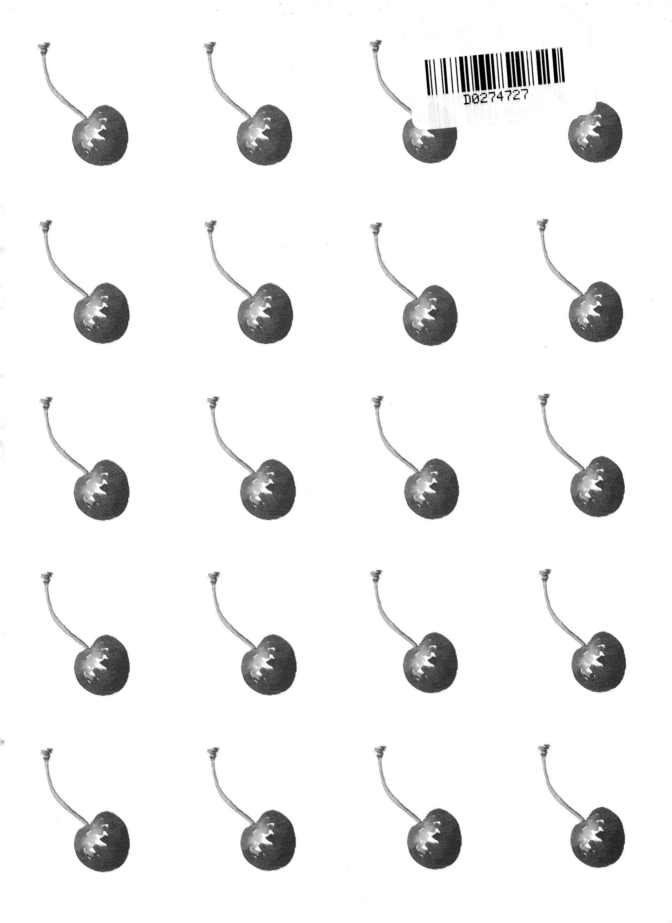

The Archers' pantry

Illustrations by Sally Maltby

over 100 recipes from Ambridge

ANGELA PIPER

as

JENNIFER ALDRIDGE

EBURY PRESS
LONDON

To my food-loving family with love

First published in 1997

13 5 7 9 10 8 6 4 2

Text © Angela Piper 1997
Illustrations © Sally Maltby 1997

Based on the BBC Radio series 'The Archers'. 'The Archers' is a trade mark of the BBC.

First published in the United Kingdom in 1997 by Ebury Press, Random House,
20 Vauxhall Bridge Road, London SW1V 2SA

Random House Australia (Pty) Limited, 20 Alfred Street, Milsons Point, Sydney,
New South Wales 2061, Australia

Random House New Zealand Limited, 18 Poland Road, Glenfield, Auckland 10, New Zealand

Random House South Africa (Pty) Limited, Endulini, 5a Jubilee Road, Parktown 2193,
South Africa

Random House UK Limited Reg. No. 954009

A CIP catalogue record for this book is available from the British Library.

ISBN 0 09 185407 5

Designed by Vanessa Courtier
Edited by Jane Middleton

Printed and bound in Portugal by Printer Portuguesa

AUTHOR'S ACKNOWLEDGEMENTS
I would like to express my gratitude to Vanessa Whitburn and Owen Bentley at the BBC and Denise Bates at Ebury Press for their enthusiastic support, to Simon Trewin, my agent, for his good-natured reassurance, and to Jane Middleton for her culinary advice.

I would especially like to thank Sally Maltby, whose drawings delight me, my husband Peter, who deciphered my untidy scrawl, The Archers team and all the inhabitants of Ambridge who so kindly allowed me access to their pantries.

Contents

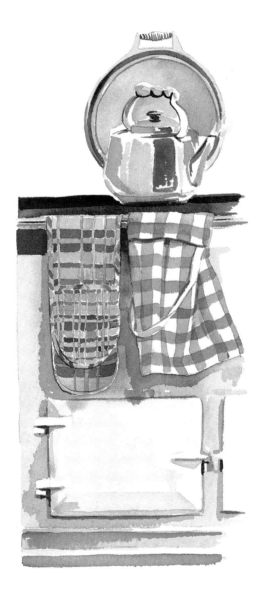

Introduction

Stop, please! It won't take a moment, I promise. Slide your silvery gliding trolley to the side. Pop your 'boil-in-the-bag-in-a-matter-of-minutes' back on the shelf and follow me.

We'll take the train to Hollerton Junction and then a short bumpy ride in Wharton's bus and we're very nearly there. Pass the mooing and clucking in the farmyard, just don't forget to shut the gate behind you, and on through the warm kitchen. There beyond the low white door you'll find it all hiding. Gathered and garnered, potted and bottled, secretly and silently stored. Tread gingerly down the worn stone steps. You can just make out, in the pallid northern light, the lumpy hessian bags bulging with early potatoes, the willow-wicker baskets wedged with earthy vegetables, the frilly carrot-tops flopping across sternly striped marrows, spinach leaves, green and silky, sprawling across crinkly grey cabbages and beans salting in bulky tubs. Smell the mellow muskiness of apples ranged in russet rows, picked on glorious golden days. See that gleaming fruit cake, Gran's special for Brookfield's Sunday tea, smelling of spices and studded with almonds, and her batch of cooling cottage loaves. Perched above, on ever narrowing shelves, are pot upon chubby pot of Auntie Pru's chutneys, pickles and jellies. A colourful jumble of tall, slim bottles of cordials jostle along jovially with the Larkin's amber marmalade, Jill's runny honey and Martha's homemade jam. Dangling from ham-hooks on a beam are strings of onions, pearl-skinned and raffia-strung and twizzling, bristling bunches of drying herbs – sage, sweet marjoram and ageless thyme. And hanging there too is an Underwoods' bag on the back of the door. Take it, please do, and fill it with whatever you choose of the Ambridge harvest in *The Archers' Pantry* – our cornucopia of the country year.

Jennifer Aldridge

AMBRIDGE PRESERVES

Autumn is upon us — heavy-beaded dew, misty mornings and golden afternoons bestow the countryside's seasonal bounty. Along the Little Croxley Lane, bee-droning hedgerows are bedecked with gleaming, tawny berries. Plums hang plump and ripe in ladder-leaning orchards, while wicker baskets brim with crisp, green apples. This glorious glut is transformed in bubbling pans to claret-coloured jellies, chunky chutneys and syrupy jam. A veritable kaleidoscope of colourful globes arranged in regimented rows on Ambridge pantry shelves.

AUNTIE PRU'S TIPS FOR PERFECT PICKLES AND JAMS

• NEVER USE A COPPER OR BRASS PRESERVING PAN FOR CHUTNEYS AND PICKLES — IT'LL GIVE THEM A METALLIC TASTE.

• USE A STAINLESS STEEL KNIFE FOR CHOPPING FRUIT AND VEGETABLES. STIR WITH WOODEN SPOONS.

• NEVER MAKE JAM WITH OVERRIPE FRUIT.

• TO STERILIZE JARS AND BOTTLES, WASH THEM IN HOT SOAPY WATER, RINSE WELL AND DRY ON A CLEAN CLOTH, THEN PLACE IN A LOW OVEN. FILL THE JARS WHILE HOT.

• PACK DOWN THE PRESERVES IN THE JARS TO REMOVE AIR BUBBLES. SEAL WHEN THE CONTENTS ARE PIPING HOT OR COMPLETELY COLD — NEVER LUKEWARM. DIP THE PAPER DISCS IN BRANDY FIRST IF SEALING COLD.

• ALWAYS LABEL AND DATE THE JARS AND STORE IN A COOL, DARK, AIRY CUPBOARD OR SHELF, LARDER OR CELLAR.

• MOST CHUTNEYS AND JAMS IMPROVE IF STORED FOR 2—3 WEEKS BEFORE OPENING.

Eddie Grundy's Saucy Pickle

MAKES ABOUT 2.5KG (5LB)

This savoury relish was concocted specially by Clarrie to spice up the barbecued sausages for one of Eddie's Country and Western evenings at Grange Farm.

2 large onions, chopped
2 garlic cloves, crushed
1 celery stick, chopped
2 large carrots, diced
450g (1lb) cooking apples, cored,
*   peeled and chopped*
450g (1lb) dates, minced
450g (1lb) sultanas

grated rind and juice of 2 oranges
2 tbsp English mustard or Grundy's
*   Fuggle Mustard (see below)*
1 tsp ground ginger
600ml (1 pint) malt vinegar
1 tsp salt
1 tsp ground cinnamon
450g (1lb) dark moist brown sugar

Put all the ingredients except the sugar into a preserving pan and bring to the boil, stirring from time to time. Simmer for about 30 minutes, until the vegetables are tender. Add the sugar and stir to dissolve. Simmer for another 20 minutes or until the mixture thickens. Pour into sterilized jars and seal with vinegar-proof tops while hot.

Grundy's Fuggle Mustard

MAKES 1 SMALL POT

A hot and spicy mustard guaranteed to start old Joe coughing and spluttering – but he can soon cool his throat with the remains of the Shires Best Bitter.

50g (2oz) black mustard seeds
50g (2oz) white mustard seeds
1/2 tsp black peppercorns

1 tsp ground mace
1/2 tsp grated horseradish
125ml (4fl oz) Shires Best Bitter

Crush the mustard seeds and peppercorns in a coffee grinder or pestle and mortar; they should be fairly finely crushed but still keep a bit of texture. Mix in a pan with all the other ingredients and warm over a low heat until a creamy paste is formed. Pour into a clean jar or earthenware pot and seal. Keep for 1 week before using.

Country Park Chestnuts in Brandy

MAKES ABOUT 900G (2LB)

Whether or not the wild sweet chestnuts growing handsomely in Grey Gables Country Park are plump enough to make the harvesting worthwhile, this is a good recipe to have tucked away in the drawer – and after all it's easy enough to buy a bag of glossy brown nuts from Borchester.

450g (1lb) fresh chestnuts
675g (1¹/₂lb) granulated
   sugar

600ml (1 pint) water
juice of 2 lemons
90ml (3fl oz) brandy

Slit the chestnut skins with a sharp knife and cook them in a pan of boiling water until just tender. Drain and peel carefully, removing the brown inner skin.

Put the sugar, water and lemon juice in a pan and boil to a thick syrup. Add the cooked chestnuts to the syrup and simmer for 10 minutes. Remove from the heat, cover and leave to stand for 24 hours. The next day reheat the mixture and boil for 5 minutes. The syrup should have a thick, honeyed consistency. Add the brandy, stirring it in carefully. Pour into sterilized jars and seal while hot.

Ralph and Lilian's Rumpot

On those glorious early summer days, when bees are humming and bushes are bowing low with their harvest of soft, sweet berries, it's time to pickle and pot and put away for the winter. At her husband Ralph's suggestion, Lilian would carefully layer soft fruits with sugar and generous splashes of white rum, creating a richly alcoholic dessert for chilly days, which she would top with clotted cream. Also she used the fruited rum as a syrupy sweet liqueur – both she and Ralph were frightfully fond of liqueur.

Choose any ripe, soft summer fruits as they come into season – strawberries, raspberries, cherries, apricots, plums – but make sure they are unblemished. Wipe the fruit carefully and remove any stones. Arrange layers of the fruit in a large, sterilized glass jar or earthenware crock, sprinkling each layer with granulated sugar and pouring over a generous amount of rum or brandy. Cover loosely and add more fruit as it comes into season. At the end of the summer, when the crock is full, cover it securely and leave in a cool, dry place to mature.

Mediterranean Quince Leather

MAKES ABOUT 225G (8OZ)

Julia harvested a trug of delicately scented quinces from a somewhat overgrown tree at Lower Loxley Hall. Eager to demonstrate the richness of her experience in Spain, she chopped up the oddly shaped fruits and created a delicious paste to accompany a chunk of Manchego cheese. It can be eaten as a dessert, too, dredged with sifted icing sugar.

900g (2lb) ripe quinces
juice of 1 lemon
450ml (³/₄ pint) water

Wash and wipe the quinces to remove the downy coating, then chop them (no need to core or peel) and place in a pan with the lemon juice and water. Cover the pan and simmer for 30–40 minutes, until the quinces are soft. Liquidize the pulp, sieve it then weigh the purée. Return the purée to the saucepan, stir in an equal weight of sugar and bring to the boil over a low heat, stirring to prevent sticking. Boil, stirring frequently, until the mixture becomes dry and thick. Spoon into a shallow container in a layer about 2.5cm (1 inch) thick, cover with a cloth and leave in a warm place to dry for a few days. Cut into squares and store in an airtight tin.

Brookfield's Brandied Pineapple Mincemeat

MAKES 2.5KG (5LB)

Phil decided to surprise Jill with an exciting new epicurean delight. Donning his striped apron, he chopped and stirred one autumn afternoon and created this delicious Christmas sweetmeat.

225g (8oz) shredded suet
225g (8oz) raisins
225g (8oz) dried apricots, finely chopped
225g (8oz) candied peel, finely chopped
225g (8oz) sultanas
225g (8oz) crystallized pineapple, finely chopped
225g (8oz) Cox's apples, grated (include the peel)

100g (4oz) blanched almonds, chopped
100g (4oz) glacé cherries, halved
450g (1lb) muscovado sugar
1/2 tsp ground mace
1/2 tsp ground cinnamon
1/2 tsp ground cloves
grated rind and juice of 2 lemons and 1 orange
300ml (1/2 pint) brandy

Mix all the ingredients together thoroughly in a large bowl. Cover with cling film and leave for 2 days in a cool place, stirring occasionally. Stir the mincemeat again very thoroughly and add more brandy if the mixture seems dry. Press into sterilized jars, seal, and store for at least a month before using.

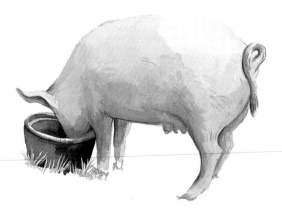

GRANNY PERKINS' EMBROCATION

PUT 1 CUP OF VINEGAR, 1 CUP OF TURPENTINE, 1 EGG AND A
SPOONFUL OF AMMONIA INTO A BOTTLE. SHAKE WELL AND
APPLY WHEN NECESSARY.

BEST NOT TO HAVE SAT NEXT TO HER IN CHURCH WHEN
SHE'D BEEN APPLYING THIS TO HER CREAKING JOINTS.

Fresh Fig and Ginger Conserve

MAKES ABOUT 2KG (4LB)

On one of her town-twinning visits to the market town of Meyruelle, Lynda couldn't resist returning with a bulging bag of sweet plump figs. 'Robert, the fragrance of France!' And what could be better than capturing that taste but in a jar of syrupy preserve to savour on a cold, grey, wintry English day? Choose figs that are not too ripe and still fairly firm.

1kg (2¼lb) fresh figs
juice of 1 lemon and 1 large orange
1kg (2¼lb) granulated sugar or preserving sugar
50g (2oz) preserved ginger in syrup, finely chopped
3 tbsp rum

Prick the figs with a needle, blanch them in boiling water for 1 minute and then drain. Put them in a preserving pan with the lemon and orange juice and simmer for about 15 minutes. Then add the sugar and ginger and stir until the sugar has dissolved. Bring to the boil and simmer until the syrup is thick enough to coat the back of a wooden spoon. Add the rum and bring to the boil again. Pour into sterilized jars and seal while hot.

Sweet Onion and Thyme Marmalade

MAKES ABOUT 350G (12OZ)

A perfect accompaniment to Point-to-Point Pheasant Pâté with Green Pepper-corns (see page 80), venison sausages or, indeed, a haunch of venison. I'm always thinking of new ways to liven up my home-grown Home Farm venison and this is stunningly simple but very successful. 'Ten out of ten!' said Brian.

1 tbsp olive oil

15g ($^1/_2$oz) butter

450g (1lb) red onions, sliced

75g (3oz) soft brown sugar

1 tsp chopped fresh thyme

225ml (8fl oz) red wine

4 tbsp raspberry vinegar or sherry vinegar

salt and freshly ground black pepper

Heat the olive oil and butter in a saucepan, stir in the onions, sugar and thyme and season with salt and pepper. Cover and cook over a gentle heat for 10 minutes, stirring occasionally. Add the wine and vinegar and simmer gently for 30 minutes or until the liquid has evaporated and the onions are soft. Pour into a sterilized jar and seal while hot. Leave for 2 weeks to develop the flavour.

Pemberton's Richly Potted Stilton

SERVES 4–6

Poor Caroline poignantly remembers this being a favourite of Guy's, with a Bath Oliver, some crisp celery and a glass of port.

75g (3oz) unsalted butter

225g (8oz) Stilton cheese, crumbled

2–3 tbsp port

large pinch of ground mace

pinch of cayenne pepper

50g (2oz) clarified butter (see below)

Beat the butter until creamy and gradually beat in the crumbled Stilton. Stir in the port, mace and cayenne pepper and mix thoroughly. Spoon into small ramekins or other small dishes and cover with the clarified butter. Chill until firm.

Note: To make clarified butter, bring the butter to the boil in a small pan, then remove from the heat and blot the froth from the top with a piece of kitchen paper. Carefully pour the melted butter into a bowl, leaving behind the milky white sediment.

Al Clancy's spicy salsa

SERVES 4

Charming, drawling Americans, Al and Mary-Jo Clancy, doing a house swap with Lynda and Robert Snell, left a few handy hints on the pinboard at Ambridge Hall – much more useful than that frightful warming loo-seat. 'Scoop up the salsa with crackers or corn-chips,' scribbled Al. And I'll have a salty Margarita with it, too. Bottoms up!

This is a cross between a sauce and a relish, depending on how finely you chop the ingredients.

1 red onion
4 large, ripe tomatoes, skinned
2 fresh green chillies

50g (2oz) fresh coriander leaves
juice of 1 lime and 1 lemon
salt

Chop the onion and tomatoes into small dice. Remove the stems from the chillies, and the seeds if liked, and chop the flesh finely. Chop the coriander leaves. Put the ingredients into a bowl and combine with the lime and lemon juice and salt to taste. Chill before serving.

Bridge Farm Autumn Relish

MAKES ABOUT 2KG (4LB)

*C*apable Pat cheerfully chops the fruit for her chutney with one hand, so to speak, while coping with 101 problems with the other – her husband, my little brother, the organic farmer Tony, being the odd one. And then there's John and his succession of girlfriends, the yoghurt, the farm shop, the cows and her mother-in-law Peggy – not to mention her sister-in-law! Poor Pat.

1kg (2¼lb) plums, stoned and
*   chopped*
grated rind and juice of 2 oranges
225g (8oz) onions, chopped
225g (8oz) sultanas
1 tbsp finely chopped fresh root
*   ginger*
1 tsp ground cinnamon

1 tsp ground allspice
1 tsp ground cardamom
2 cloves
2 tsp salt
600ml (1 pint) red wine
*   vinegar*
225g (8oz) demerara sugar
100g (4oz) walnuts, chopped

Put all the ingredients in a preserving pan and bring to the boil, stirring. Reduce the heat and simmer for 1–1½ hours, stirring frequently, until the relish is very thick and glossy. Ladle into sterilized jars and seal with vinegar-proof tops while very hot.

MRS BLOSSOM'S BLACKCURRANT TEA FOR BRIGADIER
WINSTANLEY AFTER A DAY'S HUNTING:
PUT A SPOONFUL OF BLACKCURRANT JAM IN A TEACUP AND
POUR ON BOILING WATER. TAKE HOT OR COLD. ALSO A
SOOTHING DRINK FOR DRY, TICKLY COUGHS.

Jean Paul's Green Tomato Jam (Confiture de Tomates Vertes)

MAKES 2–2.5KG (4–5LB)

This is transformed into a delicious dessert when served with crème fraîche. Jean-Paul, imbued with a fair share of French arrogance, insists it should be eaten with soft goat's cheese, a dash of rum and a sprinkling of sugar – *'naturellement!'*

1.5 kg (3lb) green tomatoes
1kg (2¹/₄lb) granulated sugar or preserving sugar
2 limes, sliced

Wash the tomatoes and slice them very thinly crosswise. Layer them in a bowl with the sugar and sliced limes, then cover and leave for 24 hours. Transfer the mixture to a preserving pan and heat slowly until boiling. Simmer gently, stirring frequently, for about 1 hour. When the mixture turns a golden colour, test for setting point: put a teaspoonful on a saucer, place in the fridge for a minute or two and then gently push the jam with your finger – if it wrinkles it has reached setting point. Skim, leave for 5 minutes, then pour into sterilized jars and seal while hot.

Mrs Antrobus's Colonial Chutney

MAKES ABOUT 2.5–3KG (5–6LB)

Thrilled to be able to explain to the *hoi polloi* that chutney is derived from the Hindustani word *chatni*, meaning a strong, sweet relish, Marjorie happily reminisces about big game and chukkas of polo, her husband Teddy's postings and their colonial lifestyle. Fascinating ramblings and a fiery chutney. Sells terribly well on the W.I. stall.

900g (2lb) cooking apples, cored,
    peeled and chopped
450g (1lb) onions, chopped
225g (8oz) no-need-to-soak dried
    apricots, chopped
225g (8oz) dates, chopped
100g (4oz) sultanas
450g (1lb) demerara sugar

1 tbsp salt
1 tbsp mustard powder
1 tsp ground ginger
1 tsp mixed spice
1 tsp curry powder
pinch of cayenne pepper
1.2 litres (2 pints) malt
    vinegar

Put all the ingredients into a preserving pan and bring to the boil, stirring. Simmer gently for about 2 hours, stirring frequently, until thick, smooth and glossy. Pour into sterilized jars and seal with vinegar-proof tops while hot. Keep for 6 weeks before opening.

Colonel Danby's Military Pickle

MAKES ABOUT 2KG (4LB)

To combat the draughts and winter chill of Ambridge Hall, old Colonel Danby and his companion, Aunt Laura, kept themselves warm with woolly 'coms' and deliciously indigestible suppers of bubbling rarebit and spicy Military Pickle.

225g (8oz) green tomatoes, chopped

2 large pickling cucumbers, diced

450g (1lb) cauliflower, broken into florets

450g (1lb) baby onions, peeled but left whole

450g (1lb) courgettes, sliced

225g (8oz) white cabbage, shredded

50g (2oz) nasturtium seeds (optional)

2 tbsp salt

2 tsp ground turmeric

1 tbsp mustard powder

2 tsp ground ginger

1 tbsp cornflour

1.2 litres (2 pints) white vinegar

1 tbsp black peppercorns

2 garlic cloves, finely chopped

Put all the vegetables in a bowl with the nasturtium seeds, if using, sprinkle with the salt, cover and leave overnight. The next day, rinse in a colander and drain well. Mix the turmeric, mustard and ginger with the cornflour and a little of the vinegar to a smooth paste. Put it into a saucepan, with the remaining vinegar, the peppercorns and garlic. Simmer for 15 minutes, stirring, until the sauce thickens. Pack the vegetables into sterilized jars and pour on the mustard sauce. Seal with vinegar-proof tops while hot.

Usha Gupta's Fresh Mango and Lime Chutney

MAKES ABOUT 450G (1LB)

Back home from shopping in Borchester's busy market, Usha unpacks a bag of mangoes. Richard Locke is amazed when she sets to, chopping the fruit and heating the spices. Soon the cottage is filled with spicy, nose-tickling smells. What's even better, the chutney is ready to eat for supper, stuffed into homemade paratha.

2 tsp coriander seeds	3 tbsp chopped fresh
2 tsp cumin seeds	coriander
1 tsp fennel seeds	3 tbsp chopped fresh mint
2 large ripe mangoes, peeled, stoned	3 tbsp caster sugar
and chopped	juice of 3 limes
2 fresh green chillies, chopped	1/2 tsp salt

Heat the coriander, cumin and fennel seeds in a dry frying pan until they pop. Put these spices into a food processor with all the remaining ingredients and blend to a paste. Spoon into a jar or dish, cover and refrigerate. It should keep for a few days.

Marjorie's Exotic Preserve

MAKES ABOUT 3KG (6LB)

Having lived so much of her life with Teddy in the tropics, Marjorie Antrobus delights in recreating something out of the ordinary – 'tasting of sunshine', she says. An excellent way of using up ripe pineapple and melon and quite delicious served with fromage frais.

1kg (2 1/4 lb) ripe melon	2kg (4lb) granulated sugar
1kg (2 1/4 lb) ripe	or preserving sugar
pineapple	100g (4oz) crystallized ginger,
juice of 2 large lemons	finely chopped

Peel, seed and dice the melon. Peel, core and shred the pineapple, taking care to retain the juice from the fruit. Put the melon and pineapple into a preserving pan, add the lemon juice and cook gently for about 45 minutes, stirring occasionally, until tender. Add the sugar and ginger. Heat gently until the sugar has dissolved, then bring to the boil and boil until it reaches setting point: to test for this, put a teaspoonful of the mixture on a saucer, place in the fridge for a minute or two and then gently push it with your finger – if it wrinkles it is ready. Spoon into hot sterilized jars, distributing the ginger evenly, then seal while hot.

Lower Loxley's Lime and Lemon Cheese

MAKES ABOUT 450G (1LB)

One of Nigel's nursery favourites, spread thickly on healthy brown bread for a tea-time treat or sandwiched in slices of Nanny's fatless sponge. His little wife Lizzie now loves it rolled inside her Luscious Lemony Roulade (see page 93).

grated rind and juice of
3 lemons
grated rind and juice of
2 limes

100g (4oz) unsalted butter,
cut into cubes
350g (12oz) caster sugar
4 eggs, lightly beaten

Put the lemon and lime rind and juice into a bowl with the butter and sugar, then strain in the eggs. Set the bowl over a pan of gently simmering water, making sure the water is not touching the base of the bowl, and stir with a wooden spoon until the sugar has dissolved and the butter has melted. Continue to cook, stirring, for about 15–20 minutes, until the mixture thickens enough to coat the back of the spoon. Do not overcook or the eggs may curdle. Pour into sterilized jars and seal while hot. When completely cool, store in the refrigerator. Use within 4–6 weeks.

WHEN STRAINING FRUIT THROUGH A JELLY BAG, DON'T BE
TEMPTED TO SQUEEZE THE BAG OR THE JELLY WILL BE
CLOUDY.

Martha's Mellow September Jelly

MAKES 2–2.5KG (4–5LB)

Martha liked nothing better on a melancholy autumn afternoon than shutting down the shop blinds and setting off on her bicycle along the narrow country lanes, hedges burgeoning with nature's bounty, then returning with her basket brimming over with blackberries, crab apples, rosehips and rowanberries, 'God's gifts,' she'd call them, 'all for nothing, too. To make jam or jelly for my Joby's tea.'

1kg (2¼lb) blackberries
1kg (2¼lb) crab apples or
    cooking apples, chopped
2 lemons, sliced
1 cinnamon stick

4 cloves
1.2 litres (2 pints)
    water
granulated sugar or preserving
    sugar

Pick over the blackberries, rinse them and place in a preserving pan. Add the apples, lemon slices, cinnamon stick and cloves. Pour in the water and simmer gently until the fruit is very soft, crushing it from time to time with the back of a spoon.

Put the fruit in a jelly bag and leave to drip for at least 2 hours or overnight. Measure the juice, then return it to the pan, adding 450g (1lb) sugar for every 600ml (1 pint) juice. Heat gently, stirring until the sugar has dissolved, then bring to the boil and boil rapidly until setting point is reached: to test for this, put a teaspoonful of the jelly on a saucer, place in the fridge for a minute or two and then gently push the jelly with your finger – if it wrinkles it is ready. Skim off any scum, pour into sterilized jars and seal while hot.

Martha's Marigold Jam

MAKES ABOUT 225G (8OZ)

Martha said she grew her marigolds to cheer up the border round the village phone box and keep blackfly from her roses, too. 'Waste not, want not,' she said as she gathered the flower heads early on a bright summer morning before the sun had started to scorch the earth. 'A magic formula to cure melancholy,' Martha assured me!

50g (2oz) marigold petals
225g (8oz) caster sugar
lemon juice

Rinse the marigold petals, removing the little white heel from each one, then pound them in a pestle and mortar, adding the sugar and lemon juice to taste, until a bright, sun-coloured paste is formed. Store in a covered pot.

Jill's Rose Geranium and Crab Apple Jelly

MAKES ABOUT 1.5KG (3LB)

Is it a John Downie? I think it is – that gnarled crab apple overhanging the old brick wall by the barn at Brookfield. I remember as a child climbing its twisted branches and peeping down through its peach-pink fruits, feeling so secure in my hiding place. Childhood memories are sweet. Now Jill, helped by Daniel and Pip's eager little hands, collects the windfalls for this preserve. It's perfect for a thank-you gift, in dainty jars with beribboned mob-cap tops.

900g (2lb) crab apples, cut into
quarters
granulated sugar or preserving
sugar

juice of 1 small lemon
4–5 rose-scented geranium
leaves, plus extra for
potting

Put the crab apples into a pan, cover with water and bring to the boil, then simmer until the apples are soft. Ladle the fruit into a jelly bag and leave to drip for at least 2 hours or overnight. Measure the juice and allow 450g (1lb) sugar for each 600ml (1 pint) juice. Place in a preserving pan with the lemon juice and geranium leaves. Warm gently until the sugar has dissolved, then boil briskly until setting point is reached: to test for this, put a teaspoonful of the jelly on a saucer, place in the fridge for a minute or two and then gently push it with your finger – if it wrinkles it is ready. Strain through a nylon sieve into a bowl. Pour into small sterilized jars, adding a small fresh geranium leaf to each one, and seal while hot.

Cameron Fraser's Tartan Marmalade

MAKES ABOUT 2.5KG (5LB)

Leaving poor Elizabeth in the lurch, so cruelly too, Cameron's legacy to the village was his excellent Scottish recipe for tangy marmalade. 'I have to say it's good,' Phil grudgingly admits, 'but the less said about Cameron the better.'

3 grapefruits
3 sweet oranges
3 lemons
2.4 litres (4 pints) water
1.5kg (3lb) granulated sugar or preserving sugar
4 tbsp whisky

Wash and dry the fruit. Squeeze the juice, then remove the flesh and pips and tie them in a square of muslin. Finely slice the peel. Place the juice, peel and muslin bag in a preserving pan and add the water. Bring to the boil and simmer for about 2 hours, until the peel is really soft. Remove the muslin bag, then add the sugar and whisky and stir over a low heat until the sugar has dissolved. Boil rapidly until setting point is reached: to test for this, put a teaspoonful of the mixture on a saucer, place in the fridge for a minute or two and then gently push it with your finger – if it wrinkles it is ready. Skim, leave to cool for 30–45 minutes, then stir to distribute the peel evenly. Pour into sterilized jars and leave until completely cold, then seal.

OLD UNCLE WALTER KEPT A SMALL STONE MARBLE IN HIS
KETTLE AND IT STOPPED THE FUR FORMING.

Doris's Dumpsie Dearie Jam

MAKES ABOUT 3–4KG (6–8LB)

'My! That smells good, Doris!' Dan would say as he scrubbed the soil off his hardworking hands under the scullery tap. It was one of his favourite dinners – Borsetshire Clanger. One end of the steamed roly-poly suet pudding oozed with this sweet orchard jam, the other was stuffed with rich mince and gravy. It was an easy way of cooking a complete meal in a muslin cloth over a steaming copper pan.

1kg (2¹/₄lb) large plums
1 cinnamon stick
1kg (2¹/₄lb) cooking apples (Bramleys are perfect)
1kg (2¹/₄lb) ripe pears (Conference are just right)
granulated sugar or preserving sugar
juice of 1 lemon
¹/₂ tsp freshly grated nutmeg, or to taste

Stone and chop the plums, then tie the stones and cinnamon stick into a piece of muslin. Peel, core and slice the apples and pears. Weigh all the prepared fruit, then put it in a preserving pan, adding 450g (1lb) sugar for each 450g (1lb) fruit. Let it stand until the juices run, then add the lemon juice and nutmeg. Bring to the boil, stirring to dissolve the sugar. Add the muslin bag and boil rapidly for 15 minutes or until setting point is reached: to test for this, put a teaspoonful of the jam on a saucer, place in the fridge for a minute or two and then gently push it with your finger – if it wrinkles it is ready. Pour into sterilized jars and seal while hot.

Poor Man's Pickled Capers

Vermilion nasturtiums clamber over the compost at Ambridge Hall. 'Pick the green nasturtium seeds on a warm, dry day,' Lynda says, 'when the flowers have only just fallen. Enliven your salads with the vibrancy of vivid nasturtium flowers or their peppery leaves. Although we may be poor, our garden is rich with offerings.'

nasturtium seeds

FOR THE PICKLING LIQUID

*600ml (1 pint) white wine
vinegar*

1 tbsp pickling spice

12 pink peppercorns

1 blade of mace

bay leaves (optional)

Wash the seeds, then drain them and dry thoroughly in a very low oven. Put the vinegar, spice, peppercorns and mace into a saucepan, bring to the boil and boil for 10–15 minutes. Strain into a jug. Pack the seeds into small sterilized jars and cover with the boiling vinegar. A bay leaf can be added to each jar. Seal tightly and leave for 2 months before opening.

Redcurrant and Rosemary Jelly

MAKES ABOUT 1.5KG (3LB)

After a long day roaming the Ambridge countryside researching local history with John Tregorran, I cooked a deliciously tender leg of spring lamb. He was such an old romantic: 'That's rosemary, that's for remembrance,' I remember he said as we wandered through the gardens at Manor Court. Carol was away at the time. Maybe it's just as well that they decided to leave Ambridge and settle in the West Country.

1kg (2¼lb) redcurrants
600ml (1 pint) water
granulated sugar or preserving sugar

125ml (4fl oz) white wine
vinegar
2 tbsp chopped fresh rosemary

Put the redcurrants in a preserving pan with the water and simmer until soft and pulpy. Put the fruit in a jelly bag and leave to drip for at least 2 hours or overnight. Measure the juice, then return it to the pan, adding 450g (1lb) sugar for every 600ml (1 pint) juice. Heat gently, stirring until the sugar dissolves. Bring to the boil, add the vinegar and rosemary and boil rapidly until setting point is reached: to test for this, put a teaspoonful of the jelly on a saucer, place in the fridge for a minute or two and then gently push it with your finger – if it wrinkles it is ready. Skim off the scum, pour into sterilized jars and seal while hot.

Auntie Pru's Cinnamon-spiced Apricots

MAKES ABOUT 900G (2LB)

Dear, gentle Auntie Pru's pantry was a veritable harvest festival – rows of colourful preserves, freshly baked loaves and flat wire racks of cooling cakes. No wonder Uncle Tom was so portly, but who could resist her country fare? Uncle Tom's greatest delight was to tuck into a generous slice of cold gammon, a brown crusty roll and spiced apricots – all washed down with a mug of cider.

675g (1¹/₂lb) apricots
1 blade of mace
350ml (12fl oz) cider vinegar

175g (6oz) granulated sugar
cinnamon sticks, cut in
    half

Put the apricots in a large bowl, pour over boiling water to cover and leave for 1 minute. Take them out, plunge them into cold water, then peel off the skins. Put the apricots, blade of mace, vinegar and sugar into a stainless steel pan and heat gently to dissolve the sugar. Bring to the boil and simmer for a few minutes until the apricots are just tender but still hold their shape. Remove the apricots with a slotted spoon and pack into sterilized jars, adding a piece of cinnamon stick to each jar. Boil the syrup until it is thick, then pour it over the apricots so they are completely covered. Seal immediately. Leave for at least a month before opening.

Wild Cherries in Brandy

MAKES 450G (1LB)

This reminds Jean Paul of the Armagnac region of France. 'Oh, to be in Gascony,' he muses.

450g (1lb) cherries
100g (4oz) light soft brown sugar
about 600ml (1 pint) brandy
a few almonds, blanched and shredded

Wash and dry the cherries and remove the stalks. Prick them all over with a darning needle. Half fill a sterilized wide-necked jar with the cherries and sugar, then fill to the brim with brandy. Add the shredded almonds. Seal and keep for several months before using.

BORSETSHIRE BAKES

Winter is with us now — a fretwork
of trees in Lyttleton Cover etched
filigree fashion against the cold,
grey, windswept sky. Bridge Farm's
organic vegetables stay earthbound
and silver-rimmed with the rime of
frost. Inside the flowery-curtained
comfort of Woodbine Cottage, an
amber glow and spicy warmth to
greet us. Floury crusty loaves
sit proudly on the pine-topped
table with glossy curranty buns and
trays of crumbly biscuits. All Freda's
fare on a typical cottager's baking
day.

FREDA SAYS:

½ TSP MUSTARD POWDER LIVENS UP AN ORDINARY

FRUIT CAKE.

Tony's Tipsy Cake

SERVES 6

A tough life my brother Tony has – organic farming is hard work without the financial reward. Well, that's the way I see it. He enjoys escaping for more than the occasional pint at The Bull but who can blame him?

200g (7oz) good-quality plain chocolate
125ml (4fl oz) double cream
1 tbsp coffee-flavoured liqueur, such as Tia Maria
3 eggs
50g (2oz) caster sugar
icing sugar for dusting

Preheat the oven to 180°C (350°F, gas mark 4). Grease and line a 16cm (6¹/₂in) square cake tin 4cm (1¹/₂in) deep. Break up the chocolate and melt it in a bowl set over a pan of hot water, making sure the water is not touching the base of the bowl. Whip the cream to soft peaks, then add the liqueur and gently whisk together.

Whisk the eggs and sugar together until pale and thick. Fold in the melted chocolate, followed by the whipped cream. When all the ingredients are thoroughly mixed, pour into the prepared tin and place in a roasting tin. Fill the roasting tin about three-quarters full with water then place in the oven and bake for 45–60 minutes, or until the cake is firm to a light touch. Cool in the tin, then turn the cake out on to a flat plate or a board and dust with sifted icing sugar before serving.

Simon's Vinegar Cake

MAKES A 17.5CM (7IN) CAKE

How could a charming man like Guy have had such a sinister son as Simon? Although Simon was once extremely complimentary about my seafood risotto. I trust he'll never dare to darken our doors again.

225g (8oz) plain flour
1 tsp baking powder
1 tsp ground cinnamon
½ tsp ground ginger
100g (4oz) butter or margarine
100g (4oz) soft brown sugar

100g (4oz) currants
50g (2oz) sultanas
1 egg, beaten
300ml (½ pint) milk
2 tbsp sherry vinegar
1 tsp bicarbonate of soda

Preheat the oven to 180°C (350°F, gas mark 4). Grease and line the base of a 17.5cm (7in) round cake tin. Sift the flour, baking powder, cinnamon and ginger into a bowl. Rub in the butter or margarine until the mixture resembles fine breadcrumbs, then stir in the sugar, currants, sultanas and beaten egg.

Mix together the milk and vinegar, then stir in the bicarbonate of soda until dissolved. Pour into the cake mixture and stir together thoroughly. Turn into the prepared tin and bake for 1¼ hours or until a skewer inserted in the centre of the cake comes out clean. Cool in the tin for 10 minutes, then turn out on to a wire rack to cool completely.

Guns and Beaters' Warming Spice Cake

MAKES A 25CM (10IN) CAKE

There are no old-fashioned hay-boxes lined with straw on the Home Farm shoot these days. Instead a flask or two of steaming-hot coffee, a snifter of brandy and some hefty chunks of wholesome fruit cake to keep out the cold on those damp December days. But after the pale winter sun sinks, and the Land Rovers return down the bumpy, muddied tracks, it's time for laughter, baked potatoes and gravy-rich casserole in the warm and dry.

450g (1lb) mixed dried fruit
300ml (½ pint) Shires Best Bitter
225g (8oz) butter
225g (8oz) muscovado sugar
3 eggs
175g (6oz) wholemeal flour

175g (6oz) self-raising flour
1 level tsp bicarbonate of soda
1 level tsp mixed spice
1 level tsp ground cinnamon
1 level tsp ground ginger
100g (4oz) walnuts, chopped

Soak the mixed fruit in the beer overnight. The next day, preheat the oven to 160°C (325°F, gas mark 3). Grease and line a 25cm (10in) round cake tin. Drain the fruit, reserving the beer. Cream the butter and sugar together until light and fluffy, then beat in the eggs with some of the drained beer. Sift together the flours, bicarbonate of soda and spices and fold them into the mixture. Add the dried fruit, walnuts and the remaining beer and stir thoroughly; the mixture should have a soft dropping consistency. Spoon into the prepared tin and bake for 2½–3 hours, until a skewer inserted in the centre comes out clean. Leave to cool in the tin, then turn out the cake and store in an airtight tin for a few days before cutting.

Freda's Borsetshire Lardy Cake

MAKES 1 LARGE CAKE

Stand on the windswept summit of Lakey Hill on a clear day and you'll see the softly undulating Borsetshire countryside rolling away to the north and east. The curling Am winds idly through an irregular patchwork of fields. Cows graze in green meadows while sheep dot the gentle slopes. Wheat ripens and the brazen oilseed rapes the landscape with its alien sulphur-yellow hue. There in the distance a toy town stands in sharp relief against the rising sun – a tiny tower dominating the cathedral city of Felpersham.

Lardy cake is delicious served either hot or cold. Maybe it's even too rich to spread with butter.

15g (¹/₂oz) fresh yeast and 1 tsp sugar, or 2 tbsp dried yeast
300ml (¹/₂ pint) warm water
450g (1lb) strong plain flour
2 tsp salt
175g (6oz) lard

175g (6oz) currants and sultanas
50g (2oz) candied peel, finely chopped
100g (4oz) caster sugar
1 tbsp vegetable oil

Blend the fresh yeast and sugar with the warm water, or sprinkle the dried yeast on to the warm water. Leave in a warm place for 15 minutes, until frothy. Sift the flour and salt into a bowl, make a well in the centre and pour in the yeast mixture. Mix to form a dough, then turn out on to a work surface and knead for about 10–15 minutes, until smooth and elastic. Return the dough to the cleaned-out bowl, cover and leave in a warm place to rise for about 2 hours or until doubled in size.

Turn the risen dough on to a floured board and knead briefly. Roll out into an oblong about 25–30cm (10–12in) long and 2.5cm (1in) thick. Dot the dough evenly with half the lard, dried fruit, candied peel and sugar. Fold up the bottom third of the dough and then fold down the top third, like an envelope. Give it a quarter turn so the folded sides are at your left and right, pressing the edges well together. Roll into an oblong again and dot with the remaining ingredients. Fold and turn the dough as before and then roll into an oblong again. Put it into a tin or on a baking tray. Brush the top with the oil and leave in a warm place to rise until slightly puffy. Preheat the oven to 200°C (400°F, gas mark 6). Bake the lardy cake for 40–45 minutes, until golden brown.

Debbie's Deeply, Richly Fruity Chocolate Cake

MAKES A 23CM (9IN) CAKE

Debbie, my truly delightful daughter and the apple of her stepfather's eye, virtually and virtuously runs much of the farm these days, with competence, skill and such equanimity that I can't think who she takes after.

225g (8oz) good-quality plain
    chocolate
225g (8oz) unsalted butter
225g (8oz) light soft brown sugar
4 eggs, beaten
250g (9oz) plain flour
25g (1oz) cocoa powder
1 tsp ground cinnamon
100g (4oz) walnuts, roughly chopped
100g (4oz) almonds, roughly chopped

100g (4oz) crystallized ginger,
    chopped
100g (4oz) no-need-to-soak dried
    pineapple, chopped
100g (4oz) no-need-to-soak dried
    apricots, chopped
50g (2oz) candied peel,
    chopped
175g (6oz) raisins
grated rind of 1 orange

Preheat the oven to 160°C (325°F, gas mark 3). Grease and line a 23cm (9in) round cake tin. Break up the chocolate and melt it in a bowl set over a pan of hot water, making sure the water is not touching the base of the bowl.

Cream the butter and sugar together in a mixing bowl until light and fluffy, add the melted chocolate and beat until smooth. Add the beaten eggs, whisking well. Sift together the flour, cocoa and cinnamon and fold into the mixture. Fold in the nuts, ginger, pineapple, apricots, candied peel, raisins and grated orange rind. Turn the mixture into the prepared tin and level the surface. Bake for 1 hour, then reduce the oven temperature to 150°C (300°F, gas mark 2) and bake for a further 1½–2, hours until a skewer inserted in the centre comes out clean. Leave to cool in the tin for 30 minutes, then turn out on to a wire rack to cool completely.

To serve as a Christmas cake, cover with almond paste and ice as usual.

DRIP A DROP OF COLD WATER ON THE JAM IN LITTLE JAM
TARTS AND IT WON'T BUBBLE OUT.

Janet's Bewildering Bible Cake

To keep her parishioners on their toes, Janet pinned up this mysterious recipe in the church porch. Marjorie Antrobus was spotted carrying a basket up the path to the Darrington vicarage. Oh dear, poor Marjorie, how she must miss Robin.

225g (8oz) Judges – Chapter 5, verse 25

225g (8oz) Jeremiah – Chapter 6, verse 20

1 tbsp I Samuel – Chapter 14 verse 25

3 Jeremiah – Chapter 17, verse 11

225g (8oz) Samuel – Chapter 30, verse 12

225g (8oz) Nahum – Chapter 3, verse 12, chopped

50g (2oz) Numbers – Chapter 17, verse 8, blanched and chopped

450g (1lb) I Kings – Chapter 4, verse 22

season to taste with II Chronicles – Chapter 9, verse 9

2 tbsp Judges – Chapter 4, verse 19

IF YOU'D RATHER NOT THUMB YOUR WAY THROUGH THE BIBLE WITH STICKY FINGERS,
HERE'S THE EASY WAY OUT:

butter

sugar

honey

eggs

dried mixed fruit

dried figs

almonds

flour

mixed spice

milk or water

Beat together the butter, sugar and honey, then beat in the eggs. Stir in the dried fruit and nuts (with a little grated lemon zest if you like), then fold in the flour and mixed spice. Stir in the milk or water, turn the mixture into a greased and lined tin and bake at 160°C (325°F, gas mark 3) for 2–3 hours.

Clarrie's Scrumpy and Cinnamon Cake

MAKES A 17.5CM (7IN) CAKE

Everyone in Ambridge must surely know of Joe Grundy's potent home brew – his Grange Farm cider which he makes from wizened old windfalls. Clarrie tipped some into her cinnamon cake one day and the result was so good she's passed the recipe on to Betty Tucker.

100g (4oz) butter or margarine	*100g (4oz) wholemeal flour*
100g (4oz) light soft brown sugar	*1 tsp bicarbonate of soda*
2 eggs, beaten	*1 tsp ground cinnamon*
100g (4oz) self-raising flour	*175ml (6fl oz) Joe's cider*

Preheat the oven to 180°C (350°F, gas mark 4). Grease and line the base of a 17.5cm (7in) round cake tin. Beat the butter or margarine and sugar together until light and creamy, then beat in the eggs. Fold in half the flour with the bicarbonate of soda and cinnamon. Then fold in the cider and the remaining flour. Turn into the prepared tin and bake for 35–40 minutes, until the cake is springy to the touch and shrinking away from the sides of the tin. Cool in the tin for 10 minutes, then turn out on to a wire rack to cool completely.

Mary-Jo's Banana Bread

MAKES A 900G (2LB) LOAF

On their return from the American trip, Robert and Lynda discovered a loaf of Mary-Jo's homemade banana bread on the pantry shelf at Ambridge Hall with a little note: 'To remember U.S. by!'

100g (4oz) butter

100g (4oz) soft brown sugar

2 eggs, beaten

1/2 tsp vanilla essence

250g (9oz) plain flour

2 tsp baking powder

1/2 tsp salt

3 medium-sized ripe bananas, mashed

75g (3oz) pecan nuts, chopped

Preheat the oven to 180°C (350°F, gas mark 4). Grease and line the base of a 900g (2lb) loaf tin. Cream the butter with the sugar until soft and pale, then beat in the eggs and vanilla essence. Sift the dry ingredients together and fold into the creamed mixture alternately with the mashed bananas. Fold in the nuts. Turn into the prepared tin and bake for about an hour, until well risen and golden brown. Cool in the tin for 10 minutes before turning out on to a wire rack to cool completely.

PEGGY'S PEPPERY WATERCRESS FINGERS
ADD HALF A BUNCH OF TRIMMED AND FINELY CHOPPED
WATERCRESS TO YOUR BASIC SCONE MIXTURE. CUT INTO
FINGERS WHEN COOKED AND SERVE HOT, TOPPED WITH
COTTAGE CHEESE.

GRANNY PERKINS USED TO CLEAN HER COPPER KETTLE WITH
A CUT LEMON DIPPED IN SALT, THEN POLISH IT UP WITH A
SOFT DRY DUSTER. 'WORKED WONDERS,' SHE SAID.

Sean's Welsh Tea Bread

MAKES A 900G (2LB) LOAF

How could we have coped without Sean? I know he runs the Cat and Fiddle but he's a charming man – helping me with the lighting at my Midsummer Festival, decorating the holiday cottages when the ceiling fell down and even painting Kate's old van. Now he's given me this delicious recipe for his Mum's tea bread. There's no end to his talents.

350g (12oz) mixed dried fruit
100g (4oz) soft brown sugar
150ml (1/4 pint) strong black tea

225g (8oz) self-raising flour
2 level tsp mixed spice
2 eggs

Soak the dried fruit and sugar in the cold tea overnight. The next day, preheat the oven to 180°C (350°F, gas mark 4) and grease and line the base of a 900g (2lb) loaf tin. Sift the flour and spice together. Beat the eggs into the fruit and tea mixture, then add the flour and stir to mix all the ingredients thoroughly. Turn into the prepared loaf tin and make a slight dip in the centre. Bake for 1 1/4–1 1/2 hours or until the loaf is golden brown and a skewer inserted into the centre comes out clean. Cool in the tin for 10 minutes before turning out on to a wire rack to cool completely. Store in an airtight tin and keep for at least a day before serving it sliced and spread with butter.

Nora McAuley's Springtime Soda Bread

MAKES 2 SMALL LOAVES

Nora, blond, bold and resolute, worked as a barmaid at The Bull. Actually she had come across from Ireland to be with her precious Paddy but things didn't work out. He left in a bit of a hurry, thank goodness! His legacy I'd prefer not to mention – and hers is this excellent soda bread, which Mum still bakes from time to time. If you can't get buttermilk, squeeze some lemon juice into ordinary milk and leave for 20 minutes to sour it.

225g (8oz) wholemeal flour
375g (13oz) strong plain flour
2 tsp salt
1 tsp bicarbonate of soda
25g (1oz) lard
1 spring onion, finely chopped

2 tbsp chopped fresh parsley
2 tbsp chopped fresh tarragon
50g (2oz) medium oatmeal
600ml (1 pint) buttermilk or sour milk

Preheat the oven to 190°C (375°F, gas mark 5). Sift the flours, salt and bicarbonate of soda into a bowl and rub in the lard. Stir in the spring onion, herbs and oatmeal, then mix to a loose dough with the milk, adding it a little at a time. Knead the dough lightly just until smooth and then shape into 2 loaves. Place on a greased baking sheet. Score the centre of each loaf with the back of a knife and sprinkle with a little wholemeal flour. Bake for about 30 minutes, until the loaves sound hollow when tapped underneath. Eat while fresh.

Little Pip's Gingerbread Animals

Jill has divine patience with her grandchildren, especially the new little bundle of joy, and now Ruth's so busy she's only too happy to look after Philippa Rose. Pip adores helping grandmother Jill make gingerbread animals. She likes putting in their curranty eyes best of all – and eating them too, of course!

350g (12oz) plain flour
1 tsp bicarbonate of soda
1 tsp ground ginger
1 tsp ground cinnamon
100g (4oz) butter or hard margarine

175g (6oz) muscovado
sugar
4 tbsp golden syrup
1 egg, beaten
currants, to decorate

Preheat the oven to 160°C (325°F, gas mark 3). Sift the flour, bicarbonate of soda, ginger and cinnamon into a bowl and then rub in the butter or margarine until the mixture resembles breadcrumbs. Stir in the sugar. Add the syrup and egg and mix to a soft dough. Knead lightly on a floured board until smooth, then cover and chill for 30 minutes.

Roll out the dough to about 3–5mm ($^1/_8$–$^1/_4$in) thick and cut out shapes with a non-fluted scone cutter or fancy cutters. Assemble the shapes to resemble animals and decorate with currants. Place on greased baking sheets and bake for 10–15 minutes, until golden. Cool on the baking sheets for 5 minutes and then transfer to a wire rack to cool completely.

STORE SUGAR AND SALT TOGETHER IN A DRY PLACE.

Christopher's Chocolate-frilled Florentines

MAKES 12

*L*ittle Christopher is a credit to the Carter family. Susan spends a lot of time with him when she's not busy working. She's a wonderful mother. Maybe she feels guilty, though. But all mothers end up feeling guilty about something, don't they? She said Christopher chopped up the fruit for these biscuits – which she made for the W.I. – and dipped them in chocolate. I think she got the recipe out of a magazine.

65g (2¹/₂oz) unsalted butter

50g (2oz) caster sugar

25g (1oz) glacé cherries, chopped

25g (1oz) crystallized pineapple, chopped

40g (1¹/₂oz) macadamia nuts, chopped

2 tbsp double cream

20g (³/₄oz) candied peel, chopped

20g (³/₄oz) raisins

15g (¹/₂oz) plain flour

100g (4oz) good-quality plain chocolate

Preheat the oven to 180°C (350°F, gas mark 4). Melt the butter in a saucepan, add the sugar and heat gently until dissolved, then bring to the boil. Remove from the heat and stir in all the remaining ingredients except the chocolate. Place heaped teaspoonfuls of the mixture on a greased baking sheet, spaced well apart. Bake for 8–10 minutes, until the biscuits have spread and are golden brown. Leave on the baking sheet to cool for a few minutes, then transfer to a wire rack to cool completely.

Break up the chocolate and melt it in a bowl set over a pan of hot water, making sure the water is not touching the base of the bowl. Stir until smooth. Roll the edges of the biscuits in the chocolate and place them on a sheet of non-stick baking parchment until set. Store in an airtight tin.

Roger's Sweet and Melting Moments

MAKES ABOUT 15

Roger Travers-Macy turned our lives upside down when he appeared unexpectedly for our daughter Debbie's 21st birthday. How could I have been so stupid and fallen for him all over again? He always was a smoothie.

100g (4oz) soft margarine
75g (3oz) caster sugar
$^1/_2$ beaten egg
a few drops of almond essence

150g (5oz) self-raising flour
40g (1$^1/_2$oz) desiccated coconut
a few glacé cherries, halved, to decorate

Preheat the oven to 160°C (325°F, gas mark 3). Beat together the margarine and sugar until creamy, then beat in the egg and almond essence. Add the flour and mix thoroughly. With wet hands, form the mixture into balls the size of a walnut and roll them in the coconut to coat. Place on a greased baking tray, leaving plenty of room for them to spread, and flatten each biscuit slightly with wet fingers. Decorate with pieces of glacé cherry. Bake for 20 minutes or until the biscuits are golden. Cool on the tray for 5 minutes before transferring to a wire rack to cool completely.

Lettie's Lavender Shortbread

MAKES 12 PIECES

Mauve and grey clumps of sweet-smelling lavender bloomed in the gardens of Glebe Cottage, reminding Gran Archer of Lettie Lawson-Hope. Lettie, to whom she was in service, bequeathed this little thatched cottage to my grandmother and she and Dan lived happily there in their retirement.

1 tbsp lavender flowers
1 tbsp granulated sugar
175g (6oz) plain flour

100g (4oz) unsalted butter
50g (2oz) caster sugar

Preheat the oven to 160°C (325°F, gas mark 3). Grind the lavender flowers with the granulated sugar in a spice mill or a coffee grinder, then stir this dark, aromatic mixture into the flour. Cream the butter and caster sugar together until light and fluffy. Add the flour and stir until the mixture binds together. Press into a greased 17.5cm (7in) round tin and bake for about 40 minutes, until pale golden. Leave the shortbread to cool in the tin, then cut into pieces to serve.

RUTH'S SAVOURY FLAPJACKS

BEAT TOGETHER 100G (4OZ) BUTTER, 225G (8OZ) ROLLED
OATS, 50G (2OZ) GRATED BORSETSHIRE CHEESE, 1 EGG AND
A PINCH EACH OF SALT, PEPPER, PAPRIKA AND MUSTARD
POWDER. TURN INTO AN OILED TIN AND BAKE AT 180°C
(350°F, GAS MARK 4) FOR ABOUT 30 MINUTES.
DAVID LOVES THEM WITH HIS CUP OF COFFEE.

Betty's Bring-and-Buy Brownies

MAKES 18

When you need help, ask a busy woman, they say, and that's Betty Tucker. Cakes for the cake stall, cleaning for the Snells, helping in the dairy, barmaiding at The Bull. She can never say no to anyone – except Brian, I believe.

*100g (4oz) good-quality plain
    chocolate*
100g (4oz) butter
225g (8oz) caster sugar

¹/₂ tsp vanilla essence
2 eggs, beaten
150g (5oz) self-raising flour
100g (4oz) walnuts, roughly chopped

Preheat the oven to 180°C (350°F, gas mark 4). Grease and line the base of a 17.5 x 27.5 cm (7 x 11in) tin. Break up the chocolate and melt it in a large bowl set over a pan of hot water, making sure the water is not touching the base of the bowl. Cool slightly. Beat in the butter and sugar, then add the vanilla essence and eggs a little at a time. Fold in the flour and chopped nuts. Turn the mixture into the tin and bake for 25–35 minutes, until the mixture is shrinking from the sides of the tin. Leave to cool in the tin, then cut into pieces. Store in an airtight tin or freeze.

Nigel's Nanny's Nursery Pudding

SERVES 6

Lucky and lovable Nigel Pargetter was cared for in those innocent formative years by a doting nanny. If Nigel was good, it was syrupy pud – and even a spoonful for Tiddles.

100g (4oz) unsalted butter
100g (4oz) caster sugar
grated rind and juice of 1 orange

2 eggs, beaten
175g (6oz) self-raising flour
6 tbsp golden syrup

Preheat the oven to 160°C (325°F, gas mark 3). In a mixing bowl cream the butter and sugar together until pale and fluffy. Beat in the orange rind and juice and then beat in the eggs a little at a time. Fold in the flour.

Spoon the syrup into a greased 1.2 litre (2 pint) pudding basin and then spoon in the sponge mixture. Cover the basin with pleated greaseproof paper or foil and place in a roasting tin three-quarters filled with water. Bake for $1^1/_2$–2 hours, until risen and firm, topping up the water in the roasting tin if necessary. Turn out and serve with a jug of warmed golden syrup mixed with fresh orange juice.

Rosie's Yarmouth Biscuits

MAKES 45–50

Clarrie's elder sister Rosie, tucked away in East Anglia, has proved to be a welcome 'port in a storm' for Clarrie on more than one occasion.

225g (8oz) butter	*350g (12oz) plain flour*
225g (8oz) caster sugar	*175g (6oz) currants*
3 eggs, beaten	*½ tsp freshly grated nutmeg*

Preheat the oven to 190°C (375°F, gas mark 5). Beat the butter and sugar together until soft and pale. Add all the remaining ingredients and stir together until the mixture forms a stiff dough. Place heaped teaspoonfuls of the mixture well spaced apart on greased baking sheets, lightly pressing them flat with the palm of your hand. Bake for 12–15 minutes, until golden brown around the edges, then transfer to a wire rack and leave to cool.

Walter Gabriel's Walnut Shortbread

MAKES 12 PIECES

Tea time at Honeysuckle Cottage: the kettle singing on the hob, the wall clock ticking and Uncle Walter's rocking chair creaking. While in the fire's glow he and Granny P. would while away the hours with many a tall story.

100g (4oz) plain flour
pinch of salt
50g (2oz) cornflour
100g (4oz) butter

50g (2oz) walnuts, very finely
chopped
1 tbsp caster sugar
1 egg yolk

Preheat the oven to 160°C (325°F, gas mark 3). Grease and line a shallow 17.5cm (7in) round tin. Sift the flour, salt and cornflour into a bowl and rub in the butter until sand-like in texture. Stir in the walnuts and sugar. Mix in the egg yolk and knead well together to a firm dough. Press the mixture into the prepared tin and bake for about 40 minutes, until pale golden brown. Remove from the oven and mark it into wedges. Leave to cool in the tin.

Doctor Locke's Dales Cake

MAKES A 23CM (9IN) CAKE

T he serious and somewhat dour Dr Locke said this is quite a departure from his mother's traditional Yorkshire cheesecake. I do wish someone could cheer him up, though.

175g (6oz) self-raising flour
1 tsp baking powder
75g (3oz) soft brown sugar
50g (2oz) raisins
50g (2oz) sultanas
50g (2oz) walnuts, chopped
2 eggs

90ml (3fl oz) vegetable oil
450g (1lb) cooking apples, cored,
   peeled and chopped
225g (8oz) crumbly Wensleydale
   cheese with apricot or
   Borsetshire cheese,
   grated

Preheat the oven to 180°C (350°F, gas mark 4). Grease and line a deep 20cm (8in) loose-based cake tin. Sift the flour and baking powder into a bowl and stir in the sugar, raisins, sultanas and nuts. Beat the eggs together with the oil and stir into the dry ingredients. Finally add the chopped apples. Put half the mixture into the prepared tin. Cover with the grated cheese and then top with the remaining cake mixture. Bake for 50–60 minutes, until the cake is shrinking from the sides of the tin. Leave to cool in the tin for 10 minutes, then turn out on to a wire rack to cool completely.

Laurence Lovell's Lemon Puffs

MAKES ABOUT 16

I imagine nothing could make Laurence happier than lolling back on his sofa listening to a sweet melody of Ivor Novello's, sipping a sweet sherry and nibbling a sugary lemon puff – but perhaps I'm being unkind.

100g (4oz) unsalted butter
100g (4oz) caster sugar, plus extra
    for coating

1 egg, beaten
grated rind of 1¹/₂ lemons
225g (8oz) self-raising flour, sifted

Preheat the oven to 180°C (350°F, gas mark 4). Cream the butter and sugar together until soft and pale. Beat in the egg, followed by the lemon rind, and then fold in the flour. Flour your hands lightly and form the mixture into little round cushions the size of a walnut. Roll them in caster sugar to coat. Place them on a greased baking tray, flattening each cushion slightly with the palm of your hand. Bake for 15–20 minutes, until pale golden. Cool on the baking tray for 5 minutes before transferring them to a wire rack to cool completely.

SQUIRE LAWSON-HOPE'S BUTLER LEFT THESE SCRIBBLED
NOTES:
TO BRING OUT THE LUSTRE OF PEWTER, RUB WITH A RAW
CABBAGE LEAF, RINSE, THEN RUB AGAIN WITH THE GREEN
PART OF A LEEK. RINSE AGAIN AND POLISH WITH A
WOOLLEN CLOTH.

WILLIAM GRUNDY'S BLACK BEETLE TRAP
PUT SOME SHIRE'S BEST BITTER IN A SAUCER, LEAN STRIPS
OF CARDBOARD SMEARED WITH ONION JUICE AGAINST IT
AND PLACE IN A DARK ROOM.

Gibson's Amazing Chickpea Bake

SERVES 4

Gibson, that gloriously good-looking college chum of Kate's, lived for a very short time in one of Home Farm's holiday cottages. They entertained us one evening and Brian and I just can't remember a meal we have enjoyed more.

225g (8oz) chickpeas
2 tbsp olive oil
2 onions, chopped
5 garlic cloves, halved
100g (4oz) mushrooms, chopped
225g (8oz) small turnips, chopped
225g (8oz) carrots, sliced

4 cloves
1/2 cinnamon stick
large sprig of fresh thyme
150ml (1/4 pint) vegetable stock
150ml (1/4 pint) red wine
salt and freshly ground black
  pepper

Soak the chickpeas in water to cover overnight, then drain. Cover with fresh water, bring to the boil and simmer until tender, then drain again.

Preheat the oven to 180°C (350°F, gas mark 4). Heat the oil in a large, heavy-based saucepan over a low heat. Add the onions and garlic and cook, stirring, until they begin to brown but not burn. Stir in all the vegetables and cook for a few minutes, then transfer to a casserole dish. Stir in the chickpeas, spices, thyme, stock and wine and season well with salt and pepper. Cover and bake for 1 1/2 hours.

Serve on a bed of healthy brown rice.

Roy Tucker's Lentil Bake

SERVES 4

A college boy now – a credit to Betty and Mike. They must be so proud of their boy's success. How did they possibly manage to help him with his homework?

2 carrots, finely diced
2 parsnips, finely diced
225g (8oz) split red lentils
25g (1oz) butter
1 onion, finely chopped
25g (1oz) plain flour
300ml (¹/₂ pint) milk

1 tsp Dijon mustard
50g (2oz) Cheshire or Borsetshire
    cheese, grated
2 tbsp wholemeal breadcrumbs
25g (1oz) mixed nuts,
    chopped
salt and freshly ground black pepper

Cook the carrots and parsnips in boiling salted water until tender and then drain. Cook the lentils in boiling water for 15–20 minutes, until tender, then drain and mix with the carrots and parsnips.

Melt the butter in a saucepan and sauté the onion for 2–3 minutes, until softened. Stir in the flour, cook for 1–2 minutes and then gradually stir in the milk. Cook, stirring, until the sauce thickens and bubbles. Stir in the mustard and the lentil mixture and season to taste. Simmer until heated through. Pour into individual flameproof dishes, sprinkle with the cheese, breadcrumbs and nuts and brown under a hot grill.

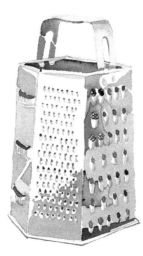

Kate's Falafel

SERVES 10

Although, as Brian smugly pointed out, it was not an amazing financial success, it was a remarkable achievement for Kate and Roy to travel the countryside in a clapped-out van, selling their spicy ethnic foods to funny fairs and folksy gatherings.

450g (1lb) chickpeas
1 large onion, chopped
3 garlic cloves, chopped
4 spring onions, chopped
1 tsp baking powder
1 tsp ground cumin

large bunch of fresh coriander,
*   chopped*
large bunch of fresh
*   flat-leafed parsley,*
*   chopped*
vegetable oil for deep-frying

Soak the chickpeas in water to cover overnight, then drain. Cover with fresh water, bring to the boil and simmer until tender, then drain very thoroughly.

Put all the ingredients except the oil in a food processor. Process until the paste is smooth but not completely puréed. Take small lumps of the mixture in your hands and form into patties 5cm (2in) in diameter and 2cm (³/₄in) thick. Deep-fry them in hot oil, turning if necessary, until golden on both sides, then drain on kitchen paper. Serve with pitta bread, Kate's Simple Hummus (see page 83) and salad. The falafel can be made in advance and reheated in the oven if necessary.

Robert's Comforting Spinach and Coriander Roulade

SERVES 6

It must be a nightmare being swept along by Lynda's forceful views and green issues. At least poor Robert manages to sneak some time with Leonie and Coriander, his daughters from his former marriage.

900g (2lb) fresh spinach

4 eggs, separated

15g (½oz) butter, melted

175g (6oz) soft cheese with garlic
    and herbs

3 tbsp crème fraîche

2 tbsp chopped fresh
    coriander

salt and freshly ground black
    pepper

Preheat the oven to 200°C (400°F, gas mark 6). Grease a 33 x 23cm (13 x 9in) Swiss roll tin and line the base with non-stick baking parchment. Wash the spinach and discard the stalks. Put in a large saucepan with just the water clinging to its leaves and cook over a low heat for 5 minutes, until wilted and tender. Drain thoroughly and then chop very finely or purée in a food processor. Add the egg yolks, melted butter and some salt and pepper and stir until smooth.

Whisk the egg whites until stiff but not dry and fold them into the spinach mixture. Immediately spread in the prepared tin and bake for 10–15 minutes, until springy to the touch. Turn out on to a sheet of non-stick parchment and carefully peel off the lining paper, then leave to cool.

Prepare the filling by placing the soft cheese in a bowl and stirring in the crème fraîche and coriander until you have a smooth, creamy mixture that is easy to spread. Add salt and pepper if necessary and spread the filling on the roulade. Carefully roll up from the short end, using the non-stick parchment underneath to help. Serve cut into slices, garnished with mixed salad leaves.

Olive, Rosemary and Mozzarella Focaccia

MAKES 2 SMALL LOAVES

The perfect accompaniment to a mixed leaf salad supper by our limpid pool, with a glass or two of something chilled and white to settle the dust of harvesting. A supremely relaxing end to a farmer's tiring day.

350g (12oz) strong plain flour
1 tsp salt
1 sachet Easyblend yeast
175g (6oz) mozzarella cheese, cubed
175g (6oz) green olives, stoned and chopped

2 tbsp olive oil, plus extra for brushing
about 175ml (6fl oz) warm water
1 tbsp sea salt
1 tbsp chopped fresh rosemary leaves

Mix the flour, salt and yeast together in a bowl, stir in the mozzarella and olives and make a well in the centre. Add the olive oil and enough water to make a soft but manageable dough. Turn this out on to a floured board and knead lightly for 5–8 minutes, until smooth and elastic, flouring your hands as necessary to prevent the dough sticking. Shape the dough into 2 round flat loaves about 1cm (½in) thick. Place the loaves on an oiled baking sheet, and leave, covered, in a warm place for about 1½–2 hours, until doubled in size.

Preheat the oven to 200°C (400°F, gas mark 6). Brush the loaves with olive oil, sprinkle on the sea salt and rosemary and bake for about 30 minutes, until they are risen and sound hollow when tapped on the base.

Kathy's Crunchy Vegetable Crisps

Thoroughly bored by hearing in The Bull each day 'smoky bacon, cheese and onion, barbecued beef', Kathy thought she'd wear her home economics hat again and devise something new and healthy for her customers. Even if they are a bit cautious, Sid gives the thumbs up and little Jamie quickly gobbles them up! Parsnips, sweet potatoes, beetroot and celeriac are ideal vegetables to use.

Peel the vegetables and slice them very thinly, either with a food processor slicing disc or on a mandolin. Pat them dry if necessary. Half fill a deep pan with corn or vegetable oil and heat to sizzling point. Drop in a few vegetable slices at a time and fry for just a few seconds, until crisp and golden. Remove and drain on kitchen paper. Grind a little sea salt on them and, when cold, store in an airtight container.

COUNTRY TARTS, TERRINES & PÂTÉS

SPRING TIME FLOODS THE FLOOR OF LEADERS WOOD, KNEEDEEP IN BLUEBELLS' SHIMMERING HAZE, WHILE BUDS BURST AND SPRAY THE HAWTHORN HEDGES GREEN. FAR OFF ON TEN ELMS RISE A CUCKOO CALLS. IN MANORFIELD CLOSE, GLEAMING WINDOWS ARE FLUNG OPEN WIDE AND FLUFFY BLANKETS FLAP AND WAVE ON WASHING LINES. LYNDA'S EAGER FINGERS PLUCK FRESH SPIKES OF AROMATIC HERBS AND CLUSTERS OF THE SEASON'S FIRST NEW FRUITS TO FEATURE DELICATELY IN LUNCHTIME'S LUXURIES AND SUPPER'S TEMPTING TREATS.

Mary Pound's Cock-a-Leekie Pie

SERVES 4–6

Clad in winter woollies and tucked away in a little brick bungalow in Edgeley, that's Ken's widow, Mary. Her gravelly voice can still be heard grumbling over the fence. One of life's losers, in a way.

1 onion, sliced
2 leeks, sliced
225g (8oz) cooked chicken, diced
2 hard-boiled eggs, halved

2 eggs, beaten
150ml (1/4 pint) milk
freshly grated nutmeg
salt and freshly ground black pepper

FOR THE PASTRY

225g (8oz) plain flour
pinch of salt
50g (2oz) hard margarine, diced

50g (2oz) lard or vegetable fat,
*   diced*
225g (8oz) mashed potatoes

To make the pastry, sift the flour and salt into a bowl, then rub in the margarine and lard or vegetable fat until the mixture resembles breadcrumbs. Add the mashed potatoes and mix to a pliable dough. Wrap in cling film and chill for 30 minutes, then roll out the pastry and use half of it to line a 20cm (8in) pie plate.

Preheat the oven to 200°C (400°F, gas mark 6). Cook the onion and leeks in boiling salted water for 3–4 minutes, then drain thoroughly and layer them in the pie dish with the chicken and hard-boiled eggs, seasoning well between layers. Whisk the 2 beaten eggs into the milk, season with nutmeg, salt and pepper and pour over the filling. Roll out the remaining potato pastry and use to cover the pie, pressing the edges together to seal. Make air vents in the top of the pie, brush with milk and bake for 30–40 minutes or until the pastry is golden and the filling set.

Betty's Thrifty Tart

SERVES 4

Even after the compensation for Mike's injury, pennies are still in short supply at Willow Farm. Waste not, want not, is Betty's motto.

50g (2oz) onion, finely chopped
25g (1oz) butter or
 margarine
50g (2oz) cheese, grated
2 eggs, lightly beaten

300ml (¹/₂ pint) milk
1 tsp each chopped fresh parsley,
 chives, lovage and tarragon
salt and freshly ground black
 pepper

FOR THE PASTRY

225g (8oz) plain or wholemeal
 flour
pinch of salt

50g (2oz) margarine, diced
50g (2oz) lard, diced
a little iced water, to bind

To make the pastry, sift the flour and salt into a bowl and then rub in the margarine and lard until the mixture resembles breadcrumbs. Add 3–4 tbsp iced water and mix to a pliable dough. Wrap in cling film and chill for 30 minutes.

Preheat the oven to 200°C (400°F, gas mark 6). Roll out the pastry and use to line a 20cm (8in) flan tin or pie plate. Cook the onion in the butter or margarine until soft and translucent, then place in the pastry case. Mix together the cheese, eggs, milk and herbs and season with salt and pepper. Pour the mixture into the pastry case and bake for 35 minutes or until the filling is set and the pastry golden.

Spring Herb and Goat's Cheese Tart

SERVES 6

Lynda's god-like goats, Demeter and Persephone, nibble greedily at the greener-than-green grass at Ambridge Hall.

3 spring onions, finely
  chopped
1 tbsp extra virgin olive oil
175ml (6fl oz) crème fraîche
1 tsp Dijon mustard
1 garlic clove, crushed

a handful of chopped mixed fresh
  parsley, chervil, tarragon and lovage
3 eggs, beaten
175g (6oz) goat's cheese, rind
  removed
salt and freshly ground black pepper

FOR THE PASTRY

225g (8oz) plain flour
pinch of salt
100g (4oz) butter, diced

1 egg yolk
a little iced water,
  to bind

To make the pastry, sift the flour and salt into a bowl and rub in the butter, then add the egg yolk and enough iced water to make a reasonably firm dough. Wrap in cling film and chill for 30 minutes. Preheat the oven to 200°C (400°F, gas mark 6).

Roll out the pastry and use to line a 23cm (9in) loose-bottomed flan tin. Cover with greaseproof paper, fill with baking beans and bake blind for 15–20 minutes. Remove from the oven, take out the paper and beans and leave to cool.

Meanwhile, sweat the spring onions gently in the olive oil in a heavy-based pan until they are soft but not browned. Add the crème fraîche and mustard and bring to the boil, then add the garlic, herbs and some salt and pepper to taste. Cool this mixture slightly, then add it to the beaten eggs and mix together thoroughly.

Crumble the goat's cheese into the pastry shell and pour the cream mixture over the top. Bake at 200°C (400°F, gas mark 6) for about 20–25 minutes, until puffed up and golden brown.

Nelson's Criss-Cross Salmon Tart

SERVES 6

Escape through an archway from Borchester's mêlée into the market town's haven. Nelson's Café Bar dispenses hospitality with stylish charm and a certain elegance. It's a shoppers' heaven. Serve this tart warm, with a sauce of fromage frais whipped together with lemon juice, chopped dill and parsley.

25g (1oz) fresh breadcrumbs
4 tbsp milk, plus extra for brushing
25g (1oz) butter
1/2 onion, finely chopped
2 hard-boiled eggs, chopped
350g (12oz) cooked salmon, boned and flaked

4 tbsp extra virgin olive oil
1 tbsp lemon juice
2 tsp finely chopped fresh dill
2 tbsp finely chopped fresh parsley
salt and freshly ground black pepper

FOR THE PASTRY

225g (8oz) plain flour
pinch of salt
100g (4oz) chilled butter

100g (4oz) Cheddar cheese, finely grated
a little iced water, to bind

To make the pastry, sift the flour and salt into a bowl, then grate in the butter and rub it in with your fingertips. Stir in the grated cheese and enough iced water to make a firm dough. Wrap in cling film and chill for 30 minutes. Preheat the oven to 200°C (400°F, gas mark 6).

Meanwhile, put the breadcrumbs to soak in the milk. Melt the butter in a small pan and gently cook the onion until soft, then remove from the heat. Mix the onion and butter with the hard-boiled eggs, flaked fish, soaked breadcrumbs, olive oil, lemon juice and herbs. Season to taste.

Roll out about two-thirds of the pastry and use to line a 23cm (9in) flan tin. Spoon the filling into the pastry case and spread level. Roll out the remaining pastry and cut it into long, thin strips. Use these to make a lattice over the pie, pressing the edges together well to seal. Brush the pastry with milk and bake for 15 minutes, then reduce the oven temperature to 180°C (350°F, gas mark 4) and bake for a further 15–20 minutes, until the pastry is a deep golden colour.

Mrs Pemberton's Provençal Pie

SERVES 6

Caroline Pemberton, née Bone, seemingly a descendant of British aristocracy, descended yet again to find herself managing Grey Gables Country Club with disarming efficiency. She has learned a great deal from Jean Paul's Gallic kitchen and his professional Provençal cuisine.

2 aubergines, diced	*1 tbsp tomato paste*
olive oil for frying	*a few sprigs of fresh thyme*
4 courgettes, diced	*small handful of fresh basil leaves*
1 large red pepper, seeded and sliced	*2 bay leaves*
2 onions, sliced	*10 sheets of filo pastry*
5 tomatoes, skinned and chopped	*50g (2oz) butter, melted*
2 garlic cloves, crushed	*salt and freshly ground black pepper*

Put the diced aubergines in a colander, sprinkle them liberally with salt and leave for an hour. Rinse away the bitter juices and dry the aubergines on kitchen paper. Heat a good layer of olive oil in a large frying pan and fry the aubergines until golden, then remove from the pan. Add a little more oil if necessary and fry the courgettes until golden, then remove them from the pan, too. Fry the red pepper and onions until the onions are translucent and soft, adding the tomatoes shortly before the end of cooking. Transfer all the vegetables to a large saucepan, stir in the garlic, tomato paste, a few tablespoons of water and the herbs. Season to taste, then cover and simmer for 20–30 minutes, stirring from time to time, until the vegetables are tender but not mushy. Leave to cool.

Preheat the oven to 190°C (375°F, gas mark 5). Use half the filo sheets to line a 23cm (9in) springform cake tin or loose-based tart tin, brushing melted butter between each layer. Spoon the cooled vegetable mixture into the pastry case, then place the remaining pastry sheets loosely on top, brushing each one with butter again. Fold the edges of the lower sheets up over the top sheets and brush with more melted butter. Bake for 25–30 minutes, until the pastry is golden and crisp. Serve warm.

Home Farm Game Pie

SERVES 8

If my freezer hadn't been full of John's conservation-grade pork I would have used venison in this pie – cut in smaller chunks and marinated in red wine overnight.

450g (1lb) pork, cut into 2.5cm (1in) cubes

450g (1lb) boned pheasant, cut into 2.5cm (1in) cubes

1 tbsp plain flour

2 tsp chopped fresh thyme

2 tbsp orange marmalade

grated rind of 1 lemon

4 tbsp Madeira

450g (1lb) ham, cut into 2.5cm (1in) cubes

4 tbsp chopped fresh parsley

1 tsp freshly grated nutmeg

1 egg yolk beaten with 1 tbsp water, to glaze

salt and freshly ground black pepper

FOR THE HOT WATER CRUST PASTRY

450g (1lb) plain flour

1 tsp salt

225g (8oz) lard

150ml (¼ pint) water

To make the pastry, sift the flour and salt into a bowl and make a well in the centre. Put the lard into a saucepan with the water, heat until just boiling, then tip into the flour, stirring with a wooden spoon. Beat to form a smooth dough, then turn on to a floured surface and knead gently for a minute. Cover and leave for 30 minutes.

Meanwhile, prepare the filling: mix together the pork, pheasant, flour, thyme, marmalade, lemon rind and Madeira. Season with salt and pepper. In a separate bowl mix together the ham, parsley and nutmeg and season to taste.

Preheat the oven to 220°C (425°F, gas mark 7). Roll out three-quarters of the pastry and use to line a 900g (2lb) loaf tin. Spoon half the pork and pheasant mixture into the tin and press down lightly. Cover with the ham mixture and arrange the remaining pork and pheasant on top, pressing down to fill the tin. Dampen the pastry edges with a little water. Roll out the remaining pastry to form a lid, put it on top of the pie and press the edges together to seal. Make small vents along the top of the pie, then bake in the centre of the oven for 15 minutes. Brush the top of the pie with the egg yolk glaze, then lower the temperature to 180°C (350°F, gas mark 4) and continue cooking for 1½ hours. Leave to cool completely, then chill (overnight if possible) before turning out on to a serving plate.

Pat's Pork and Apricot Picnic Pies

MAKES 8

There's plenty of John's organic pork at Bridge Farm for Pat to create a delicious filling for these little pack-a-snack meat pies. Perfect for Market Day elevenses with a flask of coffee. Or ideal served warm for supper, especially with creamed celeriac.

1 tbsp sunflower oil
1 onion, finely chopped
450g (1lb) pork fillet, trimmed and
  diced
100g (4oz) no-need-to-soak dried
  apricots, chopped

2 plump garlic cloves, finely chopped
a few fresh sage leaves, chopped, or
  1 tsp dried sage
1 leek, finely chopped
1 egg, beaten, to glaze
salt and freshly ground black pepper

FOR THE HOT WATER CRUST PASTRY

450g (1lb) plain flour
1 tsp salt

200g (7oz) lard
200ml (7fl oz) water

To make the pastry, sift the flour and salt together in a bowl and make a well in the centre. In a saucepan, melt the lard in the water, bring to the boil, then pour into the well. Beat the mixture to a soft dough and knead for a minute. Cover and leave for 30 minutes for the dough to become more elastic.

Meanwhile, make the filling. Heat the oil in a large frying pan and fry the onion until soft but not brown. Add the meat and fry until brown, then add the apricots, garlic and sage, cover and cook gently for 10 minutes. Finally stir in the leek and some salt and pepper and cook for a further 5 minutes. Turn out on to a plate to cool.

Preheat the oven to 180°C (350°F, gas mark 4). Divide the pastry into 8 pieces and roll out two-thirds of each to line eight 10cm (4in) flan tins. Roll out each remaining third to form pastry lids. Spoon the cooled mixture into each tin. Moisten the edges of the pastry lids and use to cover the pies, pressing the edges together to seal. Brush with the beaten egg and pierce a hole in the centre of each pie. Bake for 30–40 minutes, until golden brown.

Nelson's Naughty But Nice 'n' Creamy Flan

SERVES 6–8

Smooth and seductive – like Nelson himself – with just the merest hint of alcohol.

150ml (¹/₄ pint) double
cream
100g (4oz) caster sugar
2 tbsp brandy

175g (6oz) full-fat cream cheese
grated rind of 1 orange
225g (8oz) no-need-to-soak dried
apricots, chopped

FOR THE CRUST

350g (12oz) plain chocolate
sweetmeal biscuits
75g (3oz) butter

50g (2oz) good-quality plain
chocolate, plus extra to decorate
50g (2oz) toasted almonds, chopped

To make the crust, put the biscuits in a large plastic bag and crush them to crumbs with a rolling pin, or crush them in a food processor. Melt the butter and chocolate in a bowl set over a pan of simmering water, making sure the water is not touching the base of the bowl. Remove from the heat and stir in the biscuit crumbs and chopped almonds. Press the mixture as firmly as possible over the base and up the sides of a 23cm (9in) springform cake tin. Put this in the refrigerator for 30 minutes or so to harden.

Whip the cream with the sugar and brandy and then beat in the cream cheese and orange rind. Fold in the chopped apricots and fill the flan case with the mixture. Decorate with grated chocolate and chill before serving.

Chocolate Pye in Orange Crust

SERVES 6

*J*ill always makes a special orange pastry for her Christmas mince pies but some-
times she uses it with this rich chocolate filling instead. There are plates held out
for seconds when she bakes this tart for a family Sunday lunch at Brookfield.

2 tbsp lemon jelly marmalade

*50g (2oz) good-quality plain
chocolate*

100g (4oz) butter

75g (3oz) caster sugar

3 eggs, separated

*75g (3oz) fine fresh
breadcrumbs*

FOR THE ORANGE PASTRY

225g (8oz) plain flour

1 tbsp icing sugar

150g (5oz) unsalted butter, diced

1 egg yolk

grated rind of 1 orange

2 tbsp orange juice

To make the pastry, sift the flour and icing sugar into a bowl and rub in the butter
until the mixture resembles breadcrumbs. Beat the egg yolk with the orange rind
and juice. Make a well in the flour and pour in the egg yolk mixture, then stir
together to make a dough, adding more orange juice if necessary. Wrap in cling film
and chill for 30 minutes.

Preheat the oven to 190°C (375°F, gas mark 5). Roll out the pastry and use to
line a 23cm (9in) loose-bottomed flan tin. Cover with greaseproof paper, fill with
baking beans and bake blind for 15–20 minutes, until pale golden. Remove from the
oven, take out the paper and beans and leave to cool. Reduce the oven temperature
to 180°C (350°F, gas mark 4).

Gently heat the lemon jelly marmalade in a small pan with a tablespoon of
water, stirring until smooth. Brush it over the base of the pastry case.

Melt the chocolate in a bowl set over a pan of hot water, making sure the water
is not touching the base of the bowl. Remove from the heat. Cream the butter with
the sugar until light and fluffy, then beat in the egg yolks and melted chocolate.
Fold in the breadcrumbs. In a separate bowl, whisk the egg whites until they form
soft peaks. Beat about a quarter of the whites into the chocolate mixture to loosen
it and then fold in the rest with a wooden spoon. Spoon the filling into the pastry
case and spread it level. Bake for 20–25 minutes, until the filling springs back when
pressed gently. Serve warm, with whipped cream or ice cream.

Emma Carter's Chocolate Crunch Pie

SERVES 12

Emma's a good, helpful girl, specially when she wants a new pair of trainers, but there were an awful lot of crumbs on the kitchen floor after she let Christopher crush the biscuits for this crunchy pudding.

350g (12oz) good-quality plain
*   chocolate*
175g (6oz) unsalted butter
50g (2oz) digestive biscuits, crushed
50g (2oz) ginger biscuits, crushed

50g (2oz) glacé pineapple, chopped
50g (2oz) glacé cherries, halved
50g (2oz) candied peel, chopped
50g (2oz) no-need-to-soak dried
*   apricots, chopped*

Break up the chocolate and melt it with the butter in a large bowl set over a pan of simmering water, making sure the water is not touching the base of the bowl. Stir in the biscuits and chopped dried fruits. Spoon the mixture into a lined shallow 20cm (8in) round cake tin. Spread it evenly, pressing down well, and cover with cling film or foil. Chill for several hours until firm. Cut into small slices to serve.

Mandy Beesborough's Red-Berried Tart

SERVES 8

Brian has always had a strange weakness for flaming redheads and horsey Mandy Beesborough proved to be no exception.

3 tbsp redcurrant jelly
300ml (¹/₂ pint) crème fraîche
225g (8oz) fresh raspberries

225g (8oz) fresh strawberries
fresh mint leaves,
  to decorate

FOR THE PASTRY

150g (5oz) unsalted
  butter
75g (3oz) caster sugar

¹/₂ tsp almond essence
1 tbsp water
225g (8oz) plain flour

To make the pastry, melt the butter in a heavy-based saucepan and add the sugar, letting it dissolve but not boil. Remove from the heat, add the almond essence and water and gradually work in the flour to make a dough. Press the dough with your fingers over the base (not up the sides) of a buttered 25cm (10in) loose-bottomed flan tin. Prick the base and chill for 15 minutes. Preheat the oven to 160°C (325°F, gas mark 3).

Bake the pastry for about 20 minutes, watching it carefully towards the end as it burns easily. When it is pale golden, remove from the oven and leave to cool.

Melt the redcurrant jelly in a small pan over a low heat and brush a thin layer of it over the pastry. Leave for a few minutes, then spread with the crème fraîche. Arrange the berries in a pattern over the cream and brush with the remaining red-currant jelly to glaze. Garnish with mint leaves and serve in a pool of Red Berry Coulis (see below).

Red Berry Coulis Whizz 225g (8oz) mixed strawberries and raspberries in a blender. Strain through a sieve, then stir in ¹/₂ teaspoon of lemon juice and (75g) 3oz caster sugar, or to taste.

Madame Beguet's Tarte aux Poires

SERVES 6–8

Peggy and Jack returned from Meyruelle on their first town-twinning visit with this recipe personally handwritten by Madame Beguet, one of the French delegation. It can be made with peaches, apricots or apples, too – at least that's what Mum thought she said.

90g (3¹/₂oz) butter

90g (3¹/₂oz) caster sugar, plus
   1 tbsp for the topping

2 eggs

1 tbsp Calvados or brandy

100g (3¹/₂oz) ground almonds

25g (1oz) plain flour, sifted

4 large pears, peeled, cored and
   sliced

1 tbsp lemon juice

FOR THE PASTRY

225g (8oz) plain flour

1 tbsp icing sugar

150g (5oz) butter, diced

1 egg yolk

1 tbsp iced water

To make the pastry, sift the flour and icing sugar into a mixing bowl and then rub in the butter until the mixture resembles breadcrumbs. Make a well in the centre and add the egg yolk mixed with the water. Combine the ingredients with a fork, knead briefly to form a dough and then wrap in cling film and chill for 30 minutes. Roll out and use to line a 25cm (10in) loose-bottomed flan tin. Preheat the oven to 200°C (400°F, gas mark 6).

For the filling, cream the butter and sugar together until light and fluffy, then beat in the eggs and the Calvados or brandy. Fold in the ground almonds and sifted flour. Spread two-thirds of this mixture in the pastry case. Place the pear slices in a circular pattern on top and then use the remaining mixture to fill the gaps. Bake for 10 minutes, then lower the oven temperature to 160°C (325°F, gas mark 3) and bake for 20 minutes longer. Sprinkle on the lemon juice and the tablespoon of caster sugar and bake for a further 10 minutes to caramelize the top. Serve hot or cold, with crème fraîche or cream whipped together with a dash of Calvados.

Freda Fry's Pumpkin Pie with Walnut Crust

SERVES 4–6

*B*ert Fry's prized and pampered monstrous moon of a pumpkin was transformed by his clever wife into a sweet and luscious pie. 'Just in time for harvest supper,' said Freda, flushed and floury-fingered at the end of a day's baking.

900g (2lb) fresh pumpkin, before trimming
50g (2oz) unsalted butter
100g (4oz) soft brown sugar
pinch of salt

1 tsp ground cinnamon
¹/₂ tsp ground ginger
¹/₂ tsp freshly grated nutmeg
2 eggs, beaten
150ml (¹/₄ pint) double cream

FOR THE PASTRY

100g (4oz) plain flour
1 tbsp icing sugar
pinch of salt
75g (3oz) chilled butter

50g (2oz) walnuts, finely chopped
1 egg
2 tbsp cold water

To make the pastry, sift the flour, icing sugar and salt into a large mixing bowl, then grate in the butter and stir in the walnuts. Whisk the egg with the cold water and add to the pastry mixture. Stir with a fork until the mixture holds together, adding a little more water if necessary. Knead lightly, then wrap in cling film and chill for 30 minutes. Preheat the oven to 180°C (350°F, gas mark 4).

Meanwhile, make the filling: remove the seeds and skin from the pumpkin and chop the flesh into chunks. Melt the butter in a large saucepan over a low heat. Add the pumpkin flesh, cover and cook until soft, stirring occasionally. After 15 minutes or so, remove the lid so that most of the liquid evaporates. Purée the pumpkin in a food processor with the sugar, salt, spices, eggs and cream.

Roll out the pastry and use to line a 20cm (8in) flan dish. Pour the pumpkin mixture into the pastry case and bake for 40–45 minutes, until the filling is set.

The Bull's Best Sticky Toffee and Banana Pie

SERVES 6–8

Kathy's never lost her schoolroom cooking skills. This is toothsome and delicious and so sweet and sticky. Sid can't say how much he enjoys it for many mumbling moments.

150g (5oz) unsalted butter
175g (6oz) caster sugar
400g (14oz) can condensed milk
2 or 3 ripe bananas

a little lemon juice
300ml (¹/₂ pint) double cream
1 tbsp brandy
grated chocolate, to decorate

FOR THE BASE
225g (8oz) ginger biscuits
100g (4oz) unsalted butter

To make the base, put the biscuits in a plastic bag and crush to crumbs with a rolling pin, or crush them in a food processor. Melt the butter in a pan and stir in the crumbs. Press the mixture into a 20cm (8in) loose-bottomed flan tin and chill for 30 minutes.

Meanwhile, make the filling: melt the butter in a heavy-based pan, add the sugar and stir over a low heat until dissolved. Pour in the condensed milk and keep stirring until the mixture bubbles, thickens and turns caramel coloured. Pour over the biscuit base, leave to cool and then chill until set.

Slice the bananas and sprinkle with lemon juice to prevent discoloration, then arrange them on the caramel mixture. Whip the cream with the brandy and spread over the bananas. Decorate with grated chocolate and then chill again. Serve in small portions – it's disgracefully rich!

73

LYNDA POPS A PINCH OF CHOPPED MINT INTO FRUIT SALADS
TO ADD A LITTLE JE NE SAIS QUOI.

Shane's Kitchen Garden Striped Terrine

SERVES 10 AS A FIRST COURSE, 6 AS A MAIN COURSE

Shane serves Nelson's customers with distinctive style, slicing and scooping, stirring and spooning his sweet desserts and savoury creations.

550g (1¹/₄lb) parsnips, cored and cut into chunks	6 tbsp crème fraîche
550g (1¹/₄lb) carrots, chopped	¹/₂ tsp ground mace
550g (1¹/₄lb) fresh spinach	¹/₂ tsp ground coriander
3 eggs	salt and freshly ground black pepper

Preheat the oven to 160°C (325°F, gas mark 3). Butter a 900g (2lb) loaf tin and line the base with greaseproof paper. Cook the parsnips and carrots in separate saucepans of water until tender, then drain thoroughly. Wash the spinach, removing the stalks, and place in a saucepan with only the water clinging to its leaves. Cook over a low heat for 5 minutes, until it wilts and softens, then drain well. Purée each of the vegetables and then return them to their individual pans and heat gently, stirring, until the excess liquid has evaporated. Cool slightly, then add an egg and 2 tablespoons of crème fraîche to each purée and mix well. Season each with salt and pepper, adding the mace to the carrots and the coriander to the parsnips.

Spoon the parsnip purée into the loaf tin, levelling it to make a smooth layer, followed by the carrot and finally the spinach purée. Cover with a piece of foil, place the tin in a roasting tin half filled with hot water and bake for about 1¹/₂ hours or until a skewer inserted in the centre comes out clean. Remove from the oven and leave to cool before turning out carefully on to a serving plate. This terrine can be served with a tomato or red pepper sauce.

Smoked Trout and Asparagus Terrine

SERVES 6

With his newfound culinary skills, Phil concocted a delectable supper dish with a pound of Underwoods' fine smoked trout and a few fat spears of Jill's asparagus. 'Sparrow-grass, that's what we allus calls it,' muttered Bert.

6 fresh asparagus spears
450g (1lb) smoked trout
100g (4oz) fromage frais
90ml (3fl oz) sunflower oil
3 eggs

grated rind and juice of 1 lemon
100g (4oz) smoked salmon,
   cut into strips
lemon and lime wedges and
   sprigs of parsley, to garnish

Preheat the oven to 160°C (325°F, gas mark 3). Trim the asparagus spears and cook them in lightly salted boiling water until just tender, then drain. Remove any skin and bones from the trout and place it in a food processor with the fromage frais, oil, eggs and lemon rind and juice. Blend well.

Grease a 900g (2lb) loaf tin or terrine and tip one third of the mixture into it. Arrange the asparagus spears on top. Cover with half the remaining mixture and place the smoked salmon strips on top of that. Finally cover with the remaining trout mixture. Cover the tin with greaseproof paper and foil and place in a roasting tin half filled with water. Bake for 1 hour. Leave to cool in the tin and then chill. Turn out on to a serving plate and garnish with lemon and lime wedges and parsley.

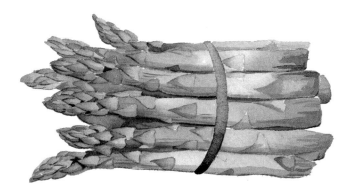

Jean Paul's Exquisite Chocolate Terrine with Crème Anglaise

SERVES 8–10

Only when the stainless steel knives are stowed away in their block is it safe to set foot in Jean Paul's secret domain – Grey Gables kitchen. With a flourishing flap of a white linen napkin, the gingham-trousered Frenchman allows me a peep at his exquisite creations.

225g (8oz) good-quality plain chocolate
1 tbsp brandy
225g (8oz) unsalted butter, cut into pieces
200g (7oz) caster sugar
3 tbsp plain flour
1 tbsp cornflour
3 eggs

FOR THE CRÈME ANGLAISE

1 egg plus 2 egg yolks   *1 vanilla pod*
25g (1oz) caster sugar   *450ml (¾ pint) single cream*

Preheat the oven to 160°C (325°F, gas mark 3). Grease a 450g (1lb) loaf tin or terrine and line the base and sides with greaseproof paper, then grease the paper. Break up the chocolate and melt it with the brandy in a large bowl set over a pan of simmering water, making sure the water is not touching the base of the bowl. Add the butter and sugar, stirring until the butter has combined with the chocolate and the sugar has dissolved. Sift the flour and cornflour into the mixture and whisk for a few minutes while it heats through. Remove from the heat and then whisk in the eggs one by one; the mixture will thicken and become slightly grainy but keep on whisking until it is smooth again. Pour into the prepared tin and place in a roasting tin half filled with water. Bake for about 45 minutes, until the mixture is firm and there is no movement when you shake the tin gently. Remove from the oven and leave to cool in the tin, then chill.

To make the crème anglaise, put the egg, egg yolks and sugar in a bowl and beat well. Split open the vanilla pod and scrape out the seeds, then put the seeds and pod in a small heavy-based pan with the cream. Heat gently until the cream is almost boiling and then pour it on to the egg mixture, whisking constantly. Return the custard to the pan and cook over a low heat, stirring with a wooden spoon, until the mixture thickens enough to coat the back of the spoon. Do not let it get too hot or it will curdle. Remove from the heat and strain into a bowl, then cover and leave to cool; it will thicken more as it cools.

Serve the terrine in very thin slices, dusted with vanilla sugar or dredged with sugar mixed with cocoa powder, with a pool of crème anglaise to compliment it.

DORIS FORREST'S HANDY HOUSEHOLD HINTS FOR CLEANING
SILVER
RUB DULL SILVER WITH AN OLD GAS MANTLE.
REMOVE EGG STAINS FROM SILVER SPOONS AND FORKS BY
RUBBING WITH WET SALT.

Mushroom and Coriander Picnic Pâté

SERVES 6

*B*efore my first child Adam was born, on early misty mornings I would walk and wonder where life was leading me. In the dewlogged grass I found a patch of perfect, pink-gilled baby mushrooms – their delicate shape perfection. It gave me such comfort seeing the mystery of nature's new lives.

50g (2oz) butter
2 tbsp olive oil
1 small onion, finely chopped
1 tsp crushed coriander
  seeds
450g (1lb) button mushrooms

50g (2oz) fresh white breadcrumbs
225g (8oz) cream cheese
2 tsp lemon juice
fresh coriander leaves, to garnish
salt and freshly ground black
  pepper

Melt the butter and olive oil in a pan, add the onion and cook gently until softened. Add the crushed coriander seeds and fry for half a minute. Add the mushrooms and toss them together briefly. They must not be cooked through. Remove from the heat and stir in the breadcrumbs so they soak up any excess liquid. Transfer the mixture to a food processor, adding the cream cheese and lemon juice, and blend until smooth. Season to taste. Turn the pâté into individual ramekin dishes, or one large dish or a loaf tin lined with cling film. Chill and then serve with hunks of crusty bread.

Julia's Potato and Red Pepper Omelette

SERVES 6

Julia learned to make this simple supper dish when visiting sister Ellen in sunny Spain. Tapas, tortillas, tarantellas ... aah. *Hasta la vista!*

2 large potatoes, peeled and diced
olive oil for frying
1 small red onion chopped

1 red pepper, seeded and chopped
8 eggs, lightly beaten
salt and freshly ground black pepper

Blanch the diced potatoes in boiling water for 2 minutes, then drain well and pat dry on kitchen paper. Heat a few tablespoons of olive oil in a heavy-based 25cm (10in) frying pan. Sauté the onion and red pepper until they are beginning to soften but not brown. Add the potatoes to the beaten eggs, mix thoroughly and season well. Pour this into the frying pan and stir to mix with the onion and pepper. Cover and cook over a very low heat for 15–20 minutes, until the eggs are beginning to set. Run a knife around the edge and shake the pan to prevent the omelette sticking, then turn the omelette over with a spatula or turn it on to a large plate. Add some more oil to the pan and cook the omelette on the reverse side until golden underneath. Serve hot or at room temperature, cut into wedges.

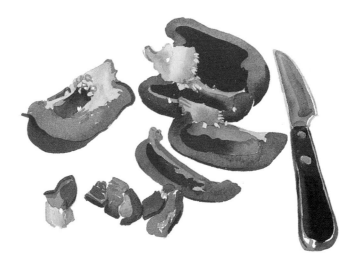

SWEET AND EASY DRIED TOMATOES
HALVE THE TOMATOES, SPRINKLE WITH SALT AND PLACE
ON A BAKING TRAY IN THE OVEN ON THE LOWEST POSSIBLE
HEAT. LEAVE ALL NIGHT, THEN PACK THEM IN JARS AND
COVER WITH OLIVE OIL. KEEP IN A COOL PLACE.

Brian's Proudly Potted Trout

SERVES 8–10

With the sensitive encouragement of his step-daughter Debbie, Brian has developed the leisure potential of Home Farm with an environmentally friendly, trout-rich fishing lake. Financially friendly, too.

400g (14oz) cooked trout
  fillets
225g (8oz) butter, softened
2 tbsp lemon juice
½ tsp ground mace

½ tsp freshly grated nutmeg
50g (2oz) clarified butter (see Note
  on page 15)
salt and freshly ground black
  pepper

Remove any skin and bones from the trout and flake the flesh into small pieces. Beat in the butter, adding the lemon juice, spices and seasoning, or blend it all together in a food processor. Spoon into a serving dish and level the surface. Melt the clarified butter and pour it over the pâté. Cover with foil and chill before serving.

Point-to-Point Pheasant Pâté with Green Peppercorns

SERVES 6

Prime place in the car park, alongside the paddock, tailgates are lowered and a picnic of dinner-party proportions has been prepared. Corks are popping and bubbles bubbling. Cheers to country life!

25g (8oz) belly of pork

225g (8oz) boned pheasant

225g (8oz) streaky bacon, rind removed

2 plump garlic cloves, crushed

1 tsp dried thyme or 1 tbsp chopped fresh thyme

1/2 tsp salt

1 tsp freshly ground black pepper

2 tsp green peppercorns in brine

2 tbsp red wine

4 tbsp brandy

8 smoked streaky bacon rashers

Chop the pork, pheasant and streaky bacon very finely or grind them in a food processor. Add the garlic, thyme, salt, pepper, green peppercorns, wine and brandy. Mix well, then cover and leave in a cool place to marinate for an hour or two.

Preheat the oven to 150°C (300°F, gas mark 2). Line a 1.2 litre (2 pint) terrine with the rashers of smoked bacon, then pack the meat in tightly. Cover the terrine with a double layer of foil and place in a roasting tin half filled with water. Cook for 3 hours, then remove from the oven and leave to cool. When cool, place a heavy weight on top of the pâté and chill overnight.

Poor Person's Caviar

SERVES 4–6

E vocatively Mediterranean, muses Phil. Imagine the sound of goats' bells tonkling down the mountainside, the smell of wild thyme, a dishful of black olives. When I retire ...

3 large aubergines

90ml (3fl oz) extra virgin olive oil

juice of 1 large lemon

2 garlic cloves, crushed

3 tbsp plain yoghurt

salt and freshly ground black pepper

Grill the aubergines until the skins are blackened all over, turning them as necessary. Leave until cool enough to handle and then peel them. Very finely chop the flesh, then beat in the oil, lemon juice, garlic, yoghurt and some seasoning to taste. Turn the mixture into a bowl and chill. Serve with Kathy's Crunchy Vegetable Crisps (see page 57).

Avocado Chilli Dip

SERVES 4–6

'W e'll need to get some corn chips or tortillas,' says our Kate, slumped on a kitchen chair, DMs adorning the table and a sink piled high with washing up. 'Don't forget to put the avocado stone in the dip to stop it discolouring.'

2 ripe avocados

1 large tomato, skinned, seeded and
    finely chopped

1 fresh green chilli, seeded and
    finely chopped

1 small onion, finely chopped

1 tbsp lemon juice

1/2 tsp Tabasco sauce

1 tbsp chopped fresh coriander

salt and freshly ground black pepper

Peel, stone and mash the avocados. Combine with all the remaining ingredients, adjusting the seasoning to taste. Cover the dish with cling film and leave for an hour or so before serving to enhance the flavour.

Kate's Simple Hummus

SERVES 8

I t's healthy, wholesome, rich in calcium and protein, Kate tells us, and great served as a sauce with grilled vegetables or as a dip with pitta bread.

225g (8oz) dried chickpeas
4 garlic cloves, crushed
juice of 3 lemons
2 tbsp olive oil
150ml (¼ pint) tahini paste

½ tsp ground cumin
½ tsp ground coriander
2 tbsp chopped fresh coriander
salt and freshly ground black
pepper

Soak the chickpeas in water to cover overnight, then drain. Cover with fresh water, bring to the boil and simmer until tender, then drain again, reserving the liquid. Place the chickpeas in a food processor with the garlic, lemon juice, olive oil, tahini paste, spices and a little of the reserved cooking liquid. Purée to a thick paste, adding more cooking liquid if necessary. Fold in most of the chopped fresh coriander and season to taste with salt and pepper. Serve in a shallow bowl, garnished with the remaining fresh coriander.

SWEET &
CORDIAL

THE STAGNANT HEAT OF SUMMER FILLS
THE VILLAGE VALE WITH LINGERING
SCENTS OF NEW-MOWN HAY. HEADY
HONEYSUCKLE AND BLOWZY FULL-BLOWN
ROSES TANGLE AND TUMBLE LISTLESSLY
DOWN OLD COTTAGE WALLS. OUT IN THE
OCHRE FIELDS, COMBINES DRONE AND
WHINE, WHILE BROWN AND BARE-ARMED
WORKERS LONG TO SOOTHE THEIR DUSTY
THROATS WITH DRAUGHTS OF QUENCHING
CORDIALS. LAZY PICNICKERS LIE ON
LAKEY HILL. THEN SUDDENLY, FROM A
LOWERING CLOUD, PLOP UPON PLOP OF
HEAVY DROPS OF RAIN BEGIN TO FALL,
PATTERNING THE SANDY PATHS AND
HINTING AT AN EVENING'S
WELCOME COOL.

Jennifer's Splendidly Rich Mocha Truffles

MAKES 24

Darling daughter Alice is still at an age when she likes to be helpful. So, pinafore-clad, she rolls the chocolatey balls in her busy little hands. Scraping out the bowl afterwards is the best bit, though!

125ml (4fl oz) double cream
225g (8oz) good-quality
    plain chocolate, broken into small
    pieces

2 tbsp coffee-flavoured liqueur, such
    as Tia Maria
a few drops of coffee flavouring
3 tbsp cocoa powder

Pour the cream into a small, heavy-based saucepan and bring to the boil. Remove from the heat and carefully stir in the chocolate pieces until they have melted. Let the mixture cool a little and then stir in the liqueur and coffee flavouring. Put in the fridge and leave to set.

Sift the cocoa powder on to a plate. Take small spoonfuls of the paste, roll them into balls in the palms of your hands and then roll them in the cocoa, coating them well. Place on a sheet of greaseproof paper and chill.

Manorfield Close's Moreish Mint Jellies

MAKES 48

A haze of peppermint floats around the winter-woolly-clad mainstays of Manorfield Close as they cluster at the bus stop on Borchester Market Day.

25g (1oz) gelatine
300ml (½ pint) water
450g (1lb) granulated sugar
1 or 2 drops of green food colouring

5 tbsp crème de menthe or
3 tsp peppermint
flavouring
50g (2oz) icing sugar sifted

Sprinkle the gelatine over the water in a saucepan and leave in a warm place to dissolve. Add the sugar and heat gently until dissolved. Bring just to the boil and simmer gently for about 10 minutes, skimming the white scum from the surface. Remove from the heat, cool slightly then add the food colouring and the crème de menthe or peppermint flavouring. Stir carefully, then pour into a dampened shallow 20cm (8in) square tin and leave in a cool place to set. Cut into squares and coat in the icing sugar.

Jack Woolley's Ginger Tablet

MAKES ABOUT 1.1KG (2$^{1}/_{2}$LB)

Fiercely proud of his Stirchley roots, his Borsetshire businesses and latter-day liaison with Mum, Jack is hard when it comes to finance but scratch the surface and he's sweet and soft inside. 'I'll never get over Captain,' he whines.

900g (2lb) granulated sugar
400ml (14fl oz) single cream

100g (4oz) preserved ginger in
syrup, chopped

Gently heat the sugar and cream in a large heavy-based pan until the sugar has dissolved. Bring gradually to the boil, stirring constantly, and boil for a few minutes until the mixture turns golden brown and reaches the stage when a soft ball forms when a teaspoonful is dropped into cold water. Remove from the heat and stir in the chopped ginger, then beat until it looks sugary. Pour into a well-greased tin in a layer about 2.5cm (1in) thick. When partially cool, mark into squares.

Mrs Horrobin's Humbugs

MAKES ABOUT 450G (1LB)

To describe the voluble Ivy Horrobin's offspring as village humbugs would be a gross understatement. But the commendable Susan Carter is the exception.

450g (1lb) granulated
sugar
3 drops of peppermint oil

150ml ($^{1}/_{4}$ pint) water
1 tbsp golden syrup
pinch of cream of tartar

Put the sugar, peppermint oil and water into a large, heavy-based saucepan and heat gently until the sugar has dissolved. Stir in the golden syrup and the cream of tartar and bring slowly to boiling point. Boil until it reaches 149–154°C (300–310°F) on a sugar thermometer, then test by dropping a little of the mixture into cold water; it should form hard threads. Remove from the heat and cool a little, then pour on to an oiled slab. Using oiled knives, fold the ends of the toffee to the centre. When the toffee is cool enough to handle, pull it into strips, twist them and chop them into humbug shapes. Leave on waxed paper to cool completely.

Aunt Laura's Nutty Clusters

MAKES ABOUT 450G (1LB)

Eager to prove her self-sufficiency, proud Aunt Laura gathered her autumn harvest from trees in the unkempt grounds of Ambridge Hall. Helped by her erstwhile aged companion, Freddy Danby, she made these nutty chocolates for a Christmas treat.

100g (4oz) hazelnuts
100g (4oz) walnuts
225g (8oz) good-quality plain chocolate
1 tsp unsalted butter if required

Preheat the oven to 180°C (350°F, gas mark 4). Toast the hazelnuts in the oven for a few minutes, then put them in a tea towel and rub off their skins. Chop the hazelnuts and walnuts coarsely.

Break up the chocolate and melt it in a bowl set over a pan of hot water, making sure the water is not touching the base of the bowl. Remove the pan from the heat and drop the nuts into the chocolate, stirring to coat them thoroughly. If the chocolate is too thick, add the butter. Place a teaspoonful at a time on baking parchment. Leave until completely set, then place each one in a little paper case.

Alice's Favourite Fudge Spread

MAKES ABOUT 675G (1^1/$_2$LB)

Alice (the apple of my eye) Margaret (named after my mother Peggy) was born in 1988. Brian was desperately disappointed she wasn't a boy. Why be so sexist? After all, Debbie's doing a man's work on the farm.

This is an amazingly versatile chocolate fudge spread. Melt it in a fondue and dip fresh fruit in it. Warm it up for a runny sauce to pour over ice cream. Or make chocolate and banana sandwiches – yummy!

100g (4oz) good-quality plain chocolate
100g (4oz) good-quality milk chocolate
100g (4oz) unsalted butter

175ml (6fl oz) can of evaporated milk
100g (4oz) granulated sugar
2 tsp vanilla essence
90ml (3fl oz) double cream

Break up the plain and milk chocolate and put in a heavy-based saucepan with the butter, evaporated milk, sugar and vanilla essence. Heat gently until the sugar has dissolved and the chocolate and butter have melted. Pour in the cream and bring to the boil, stirring constantly. Cool a little, then pour into sterilized jars and seal. Store in the fridge.

Auntie Chris's Christmas Relish

MAKES ABOUT 225ML (8FL OZ)

A succulent clove-studded slab of gammon, a baked potato and a generous spoonful of Auntie Chris's Christmas relish is just the thing for an easy meal after exercising her horses. 'Ee – that were champion,' admitted George, loosening the buckle on his belt. 'I couldn't play one single note on my cornet now, not if you begged me.' 'Thank goodness for that,' Chris whispered under her breath.

2 shallots, finely chopped

1 orange

1 lemon

4 tbsp redcurrant jelly

$^{1}/_{2}$ tsp mustard powder

$^{1}/_{2}$ tsp ground ginger

150ml ($^{1}/_{4}$ pint) port

1 tsp red wine vinegar

salt and freshly ground black
pepper

Put the shallots in a small pan of boiling water, simmer for a minute or two, then drain. Finely pare the rind from the orange and lemon and cut into very thin shreds. Blanch the rind in boiling water for 1 minute, then drain. Melt the redcurrant jelly in a saucepan, stir in the mustard and ginger, then add the shallots, citrus rind, port and wine vinegar. Season with salt and pepper. Bring to the boil and simmer until the sauce thickens – about 5–10 minutes. Remove from the heat and leave to cool. Serve chilled. It should keep in the fridge for up to 2 weeks.

Lord Netherbourne's Iced Brie

SERVES 6

Caroline's concoction reputedly came from her rich relations. It certainly smacks of style. Serve with water biscuits or with Walter Gabriel's Walnut Shortbread (see page 49).

350g (12oz) ripe Brie, soft but not runny

150ml ($^{1}/_{4}$ pint) Jersey cream or crème fraîche

150ml ($^{1}/_{4}$ pint) single cream

$^{1}/_{2}$ tsp paprika

$^{1}/_{2}$ tsp salt

Cut the rind off the cheese. Put all the ingredients in a food processor and blend until smooth, then pour into a plastic container and freeze overnight. Transfer to the fridge 30 minutes before serving.

Shula's Citrus Crème Brûlée

SERVES 6

The Grundys' beautiful Jerseys gave Shula the idea of buying thick yellow Jersey cream for her favourite crème brûlée. She was rather secretive about who would be sharing it with her. She says the citrus flavour cuts across the undoubted richness.

600ml (1 pint) Jersey double cream   *1 cinnamon stick*
finely grated rind of 1   *4 egg yolks*
    orange and 1 lemon   *100g (4oz) caster sugar*

Preheat the oven to 150°C (300°F, gas mark 2). Pour the cream into a bowl set over a pan of simmering water, making sure the water is not touching the base of the bowl. Heat gently, then add the orange and lemon rind and cinnamon stick and leave to infuse for 15 minutes over a low heat. Remove the cinnamon stick.

Beat the egg yolks and 50g (2oz) of the sugar together until light in colour. Gradually pour on the cream, stirring with a whisk until smooth. Pour the custard into 6 ramekin dishes or a shallow baking dish. Stand in a roasting tin containing enough hot water to reach half-way up the sides of the dishes. Bake for about 1 hour, until just set, then remove from the oven and leave to cool. Chill overnight.

Before serving, sift the remaining sugar over the top of the custard and put under a very hot grill for 2–3 minutes (or use a blowtorch) to caramelize the sugar.

Lizzie's Luscious Lemony Roulade

SERVES 6

It must be a nightmare for Elizabeth trying to cook anything at Lower Loxley with Julia hovering around ready to criticize her every move. Naturally Nigel was the apple of his mother's eye, so no daughter-in-law would ever have been good enough – certainly not the daughter of a local farmer! However, maybe Julia will climb down from her pedestal now that sister Ellen has 'spilt the beans' about their humble past.

4 egg whites
175g (6oz) caster sugar

300ml (¹/₂ pint) double cream
3 tbsp lemon curd

FOR THE CHOCOLATE SAUCE

100g (4oz) plain chocolate
50g (2oz) icing sugar, sifted

300ml (¹/₂ pint) double cream
2 tbsp brandy

Preheat the oven to 150°C (300°F, gas mark 2). Grease a 25 x 30cm (10 x 12in) swiss roll tin and line it with non-stick baking parchment. Whisk the egg whites until they form soft peaks, then gradually whisk in the sugar until smooth, thick and glossy. Spread the mixture lightly and evenly in the tin and bake for 25–30 minutes, until the meringue is firm to the touch. Turn out on to a sheet of parchment paper, carefully peel off the lining paper and leave to cool.

Whip the double cream to soft peaks and fold in the lemon curd. Spread on to the meringue and roll up carefully.

To make the sauce, break up the chocolate and melt it in a bowl set over a pan of hot water, making sure the water is not touching the base of the bowl. Stir in the icing sugar, cream and brandy and leave to cool. Serve the roulade in slices, accompanied by the chocolate sauce.

Grey Gables Coffee Granita and Brandy Syllabub

SERVES 6–8

Grey Gables Country Club, owned by the Birmingham businessman Jack Woolley, is set in acres of glorious parkland. It offers banqueting and conference facilities and an excellent choice of English and French cuisine in the fleur-de-lys-flocked dining room.

FOR THE COFFEE GRANITA
750ml (1¼ pints) water
6 tbsp good-quality coffee granules
150g (5oz) caster sugar

FOR THE BRANDY SYLLABUB
½ lemon
150ml (¼ pint) white wine
1 tbsp brandy
40g (1½oz) caster sugar
300ml (½ pint) double cream

To make the granita, warm 450ml (³/₄ pint) of the water and blend the coffee granules into it. Add the sugar, bring to the boil and simmer over a low heat for 5 minutes. Leave to cool, adding the remaining water. Pour into a shallow plastic container or metal tray and place in the freezer for about 2 hours. When the mixture has frozen round the edges, take it out of the freezer and scrape it with a fork so that ice crystals form. Return to the freezer and repeat 2 or 3 more times, so that the mixture has a rough, granular texture.

To make the syllabub, pare the rind thinly from the lemon and squeeze out the juice. Put the lemon rind, juice, white wine and brandy in a large bowl, cover and leave to infuse for at least 3 hours. Strain, then add the sugar and stir until dissolved. Whip the double cream into the liquid so that it holds its shape. Do not overwhip or it may curdle. Then chill.

To serve, spoon the granita into chilled goblets and top with the syllabub.

Brookfield Orchard Honey and Yoghurt Ice Cream

SERVES 8

Two busy bees together – Jill and Pat. One provides the honey from Brookfield's hives and the other the yoghurt from Bridge Farm Dairy. And we at Home Farm pour Alice's Favourite Fudge Spread (see page 90) all over it – but we're greedy.

300ml (¹/₂ pint) milk
4 tbsp clear honey
3 egg yolks
500g (1lb 2oz) thick yoghurt

Warm the milk in a saucepan, then stir in the honey. In a bowl, whisk the egg yolks until pale, then pour over a little of the milk and whisk well. Add the mixture to the milk in the pan and stir over a low heat with a wooden spoon until it has thickened enough to coat the back of the spoon. Do not let it boil or it will curdle. Remove from the heat and leave until lukewarm, then whisk in the yoghurt. Pour into a shallow plastic container or metal tray and freeze until firm. Transfer to the fridge 15 minutes before serving.

PLACE SPRIGS OF BALM BETWEEN FRESH LINEN TO SCENT
SHEETS AND PILLOW CASES.

Kathy Perks's Christmas Pudding Ice Cream

SERVES 10

This was a great favourite on the Hassett Room's menu around Christmas time. After plates brimming with succulent roast turkey and scrumptious trimmings, some people prefer a cold dessert and it's still full of the seasonal spirit.

225g (8oz) mixed dried fruit	*3 eggs*
50g (2oz) glacé cherries,	*2 egg yolks*
halved	*125g (4¹/₂oz) caster sugar*
50g (2oz) no-need-to-soak dried	*300ml (¹/₂ pint) single cream*
apricots, chopped	*300ml (¹/₂ pint) double cream*
5 tbsp brandy	*225g (8oz) pineapple flesh*

Put the mixed fruit, glacé cherries and dried apricots into a bowl and pour over the brandy. Leave to soak for 2–3 hours. Beat the eggs, egg yolks and sugar together until light and frothy. Heat the single cream to boiling and whisk it well into the egg mixture. Pour back into the pan and heat gently, stirring, until the custard thickens. Set aside to cool.

Lightly whip the double cream, fold it into the custard and then fold in the dried fruit and brandy mixture. Purée the fresh pineapple in a liquidizer and add to the mixture. Turn into a large bowl and freeze until firm. Transfer to the fridge 20 minutes before serving.

Peggy's Pink Rose Petal Sorbet

SERVES 6–8

Peggy still has fond memories of Blossom Hill Cottage – the humble homeliness of it all. The steeply dipping dun-brown thatch, its peeping windows and the garden a comforting jumble of colourful plants. Stately hollyhocks stood sentinel at the porch, love-in-the-mist spread like a shimmering, vapid haze, while the fragrance of old-fashioned roses scented the evening air.

350g (12oz) granulated sugar
600ml (1 pint) water
3 handfuls of pink and red old-
   fashioned fragrant rose petals

1 tbsp lemon juice
225g (8oz) redcurrants
225g (8oz) whitecurrants

Put the sugar and water in a saucepan and heat gently until the sugar dissolves. Bring to the boil, reduce the heat and simmer for 5 minutes to make a syrup, then leave to cool. Snip off the white ends from the rose petals, wash the petals and pat dry on paper towels. Put them in a food processor with the lemon juice and 125ml (4fl oz) of the sugar syrup. Blend to a purée.

Purée the currants in the food processor, then sieve to extract the juice. Measure the juice and add to the petal mixture with an equal quantity of the sugar syrup. Pour into a shallow plastic container or metal tray and freeze. Before serving, tip the sorbet into the food processor and blend to form a soft, pink ice. Spoon into tall glasses and serve immediately.

The Health Club's Mint and Grapefruit Sorbet

SERVES 4–6

A refreshing, rejuvenating sorbet. Nothing could be more welcome after a session in the gym or sizzling in the sauna or solarium.

100g (4oz) granulated
  sugar
300ml (¹/₂ pint) water
grated rind and juice of 1 unwaxed
  lemon

a handful of fresh mint leaves,
  preferably apple mint, plus a few
  leaves to garnish
juice of 2 grapefruit
1 egg white

Put the sugar and water into a pan and heat gently, stirring to dissolve the sugar completely. Bring to the boil, add the grated lemon rind and the mint leaves and simmer for 2–3 minutes. Strain into a bowl and leave to cool. Stir the grapefruit and lemon juice into the syrup. Pour into a shallow plastic container or metal tray and freeze. When it has almost frozen through, turn it into a bowl and whisk to break down the ice crystals. In a separate bowl, beat the egg white until stiff and then fold it into the sorbet. Return it to the freezer until firm. Serve in goblets, topped with a mint leaf.

Pat's Raspberry and Yoghurt Ice

SERVES 8

The gleaming-clean white dairy at Bridge Farm is Pat's pride and province. Skilfully she pots her Soil Association organic yoghurt for outlets near and far – not forgetting her clamouring family.

5 egg yolks
175g (6oz) honey
550g (1¹/₄lb) plain yoghurt
350ml (12fl oz) sweetened
raspberry purée

Beat the egg yolks until pale. Gently heat the honey but not to boiling point. Combine with the egg yolks and whisk until cool. Beat in the yoghurt thoroughly, then fold in the sweetened raspberry purée. When cold, churn in an ice-cream-maker, or freeze it in a shallow plastic container or metal tray and remove it from the freezer to stir from time to time. Transfer to the fridge 20 minutes before serving.

Mediterranean Water Ice

SERVES 8

A perfect and refreshing way to cleanse the palate between two rich courses – and to remind Brian of the sun sinking behind the mountains in Andalucia.

100g (4oz) caster sugar
300ml (¹/₂ pint) water
finely pared rind and juice of 1 orange
1 ripe honeydew melon

1 tbsp preserved ginger, finely chopped, plus 2 tbsp of the ginger syrup
2 egg whites

Put the sugar and water in a pan and heat gently until the sugar has dissolved. Bring to the boil and simmer for 3–4 minutes, until syrupy. Add the orange rind and juice, leave to cool and then strain.

Halve and seed the melon, then purée the flesh in a food processor, adding the ginger syrup and the strained orange syrup. Fold in the chopped ginger, then pour into a shallow plastic container or metal tray and freeze for 2–3 hours, until mushy.

Turn the mixture into a bowl and whisk to break down the ice crystals. Whisk the egg whites until stiff. Fold them into the melon mixture, return it to the container and freeze until firm. Transfer to the fridge an hour before serving.

Edward Grundy's Ginger Pop

MAKES ABOUT 4.8 LITRES (8 PINTS)

'Get out of my hair and from under Joe's feet!' Clarrie calls out to William and Edward. With a chunky cheese sandwich and a bottle of pop they're off as happy as larks, down by the stream's edge spotting sticklebacks, catching minnows and seeing the sapphire shimmer of a splashing, darting kingfisher. They return home at dusk, clutching a timid mouse-brown rabbit saved from the razor-sharp teeth of a stealthy stoat.

This ginger pop was drunk by the Grundys at haytime and harvest, and the old recipe has been handed down through generations.

3 lemons, thinly sliced
25g (1oz) fresh ginger root, bruised
450g (1lb) granulated sugar

4.8 litres (8 pints) boiling
water
2 tsp brewer's yeast

Put the lemons, bruised ginger root and sugar in a large earthenware crock. Pour on the boiling water and leave until almost cold, then add the yeast. Cover the crock and leave overnight. Strain, then pour into screw-topped bottles, or secure corks with wire. Do not fill the bottles up to the brim. Leave for at least 2 days before using.

Elsie Catcher's Early Summer Cordial

Elsie Catcher, Ambridge's village school headmistress, came to look after Lilian and me when Mum was away in hospital. Dumpy and rather dull, I thought she was, but Dad was terribly impressed by her organ playing. Mum still sniffs in a snooty way if we ever mention her name.

Pick the creamy white corymbs of elderflower early in the day. Shake any insects off the blossoms, snip the flowers from their stalks and put them in a large saucepan. Cover them with cold spring water and simmer for 20 minutes, then strain the liquid carefully through a muslin cloth. Measure it, then return it to the pan with 450g (1lb) white sugar for every 750ml (1¹/₄ pints) liquid. Heat slowly to dissolve the sugar, then boil rapidly for 4–5 minutes. After it has cooled, bottle and cork. Keep for 2 weeks before using. Dilute to serve.

Uncle Walter's Warming Winter Elderberry Cordial

MAKES ABOUT 600ML (1 PINT)

Granny Perkins simmered and stirred Uncle Walter's homemade brew, gossiping over the copper pan round at Honeysuckle Cottage.

450g (1lb) ripe elderberries
450g (1lb) caster sugar
strip of orange rind

Place the elderberries in a large saucepan with the sugar and orange rind. Bring to the boil slowly, squashing the berries with a wooden spoon, then simmer for an hour, stirring occasionally. Strain through a muslin cloth, then bottle and seal.

To make a warming winter cordial, mull with a cinnamon stick, brown sugar and a twist of orange rind. Or dilute with spring water for a cool, refreshing summer drink.

Mabel Larkin's Cowslip Wine

MAKES ABOUT 3 LITRES (5 PINTS)

Those were the days when Mabel and Ned Larkin lived in Woodbine Cottage. Holly-blue butterflies fluttered in the sunlight, lady's-smocks clothed the grassy banks and meadows were dusted with the dusky yellow of cowslips. Only the labourer's scythe and the blundering of a clumsy cow could plunder the pretty 'paigles'. 'You'll hear the nightingale sing where cowslips grow,' old Ned would say.

As cowslips are so rare nowadays they are protected in the wild. If you don't grow them yourself, gather fresh dandelion flower heads instead. Add a few raisins to each bottle while the wine is fermenting.

2.4 litres (4 pints) freshly picked cowslip flowers	675g (1½lb) granulated sugar
	2.4 litres (4 pints) water
rind and juice of 1 lemon and 1 orange	1 tbsp fresh yeast
	a little brandy (optional)

Remove the green calyx from each cowslip flower. Put the lemon and orange rind and juice in a large earthenware vessel. Boil the sugar in the water until it has dissolved and then pour it over the orange and lemon. When the liquid has cooled to blood heat, add the flowers and yeast. Cover the vessel with a clean cloth and leave for about a week, stirring from time to time. Strain off the liquid into a large bottle with an airlock fitted and leave until fermentation has ceased. Add a little brandy if desired. Bottle and cork tightly and leave for 6 months before drinking.

For a magic touch, add a sprig of blue borage with the cowslips.

Eva's Glühwein

SERVES 12

There was much metaphorical thigh slapping when Eva Lenz, our au pair, left to marry local bobby Jim Coverdale. Brian drew the line at lederhosen and his château-bottled clarets when the German Lenzs came over for the wedding.

3 bottles of cheap red wine
75g (3oz) caster sugar
2 cinnamon sticks halved

juice of 1 orange and
1 lemon
12 cloves

Pour the wine into a large saucepan. Add the rest of the ingredients and heat gently, stirring to dissolve the sugar. Do not allow it to boil. Serve in glasses or mugs.

Caroline's Stirrup Cup

SERVES 20

Served at the Boxing Day meet on Lord Netherbourne's estate – just when the foot is in the stirrup, hooves impatiently scuffing the gravel, pink jackets jostling, a mêlée of tail-wagging hounds. Then they're off – away and over the hill!

3 bottles of full-bodied red wine
1 orange, stuck with 12 cloves
2 cinnamon sticks, halved
175g (6oz) caster sugar
$^{1}/_{2}$ tsp Angostura bitters
$^{1}/_{2}$ a 75cl bottle of still spring water

Gently heat all the ingredients together in a large stainless steel saucepan, stirring to dissolve the sugar. Do not allow it to boil. Pour into a large punch bowl and serve in small glasses or mugs.

Index

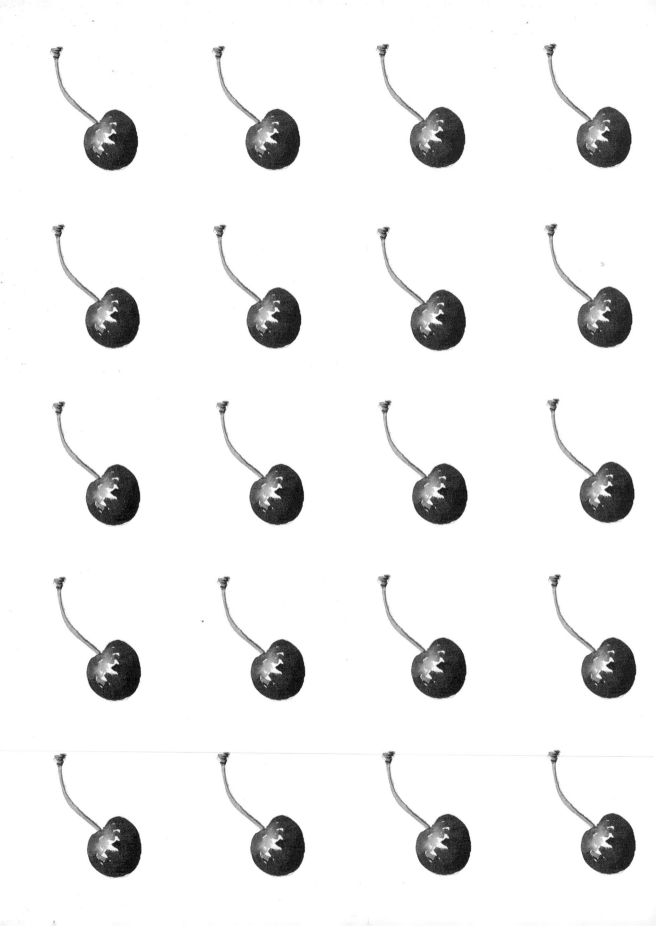